Further Communication Strategies

by David Paul

THOMSON
TM

Australia • Canada • Mexico • Singapore • Spain • United Kingdom • United States

Further Communication Strategies Teacher's Guide
by David Paul

Publishing Director: Paul Tan   **ELT Consultant:** Mark Rossiter
ELT Director: John Lowe   **Interior/Cover Design:** Lynn Dennett
Senior Development Editor: Guy de Villiers   **Illustrator:** Ross Thomson
Marketing Manager: Ian Martin   **Printer:** Seng Lee Press

For more information, contact Thomson Learning, 5 Shenton Way, #01-01 UIC Building,
Singapore 068808. Or you can visit our Internet site at http://www.thomsonlearningasia.com

For permission to use the material from this text or product, contact us by
Tel: (65) 6410-1200
Fax: (65) 6410-1208
Email: tlsg.info@thomson.com

ISBN 981-243-021-0

Printed in Singapore
2 3 4 5 6 08 07 06 05 04

Contents

The Stages of a Unit

There is no 'right' way to use this book. Every teacher has a different style and every learning situation has its own unique requirements. The following is simply a list of suggestions for teachers using the course for the first time. The aim is not to be prescriptive, but to suggest methods that can be successfully adapted to individual teaching styles and students' needs.

1st page of a unit: Lead-in

MOVIE PICTURE

It is not absolutely necessary to use the picture. Just having it there helps draw the students into the unit. However, if you decide to use it, there are various techniques that can be used. Much depends on the level of the students, how much they know about movies, and on whether they will speak out at this stage without having any text to help them. With all these activities, the students should be encouraged to speak but not corrected too heavily.

Here are a few ideas:

Movies
Ask the students if any of them have seen the movie. If one or more have, encourage them to tell the others what they can remember about it.

Actors
If the students recognize the actors, encourage them to tell the rest of the class about them, and see if they know of any other movies they have been in. They could also say something about these other movies.

Writing first thoughts
Ask the students to write down three things that occur to them when they look at the picture. Then, in pairs, the students take turns to ask each other why they wrote down each of the three points.

Project
Have the students find out as much as possible about the movie either before the lesson or after the first lesson on the unit. They can then report back what they find. They can all give a general report, or different students can be assigned different tasks such as to find out about the plot, the actors, where it was filmed, the theme music etc...

WARM-UP QUESTIONS

Either ask individual students the questions, have them ask and answer in pairs, have them write down short answers to each question before talking, or just write down their answers and not talk at all. This is only a warm-up so don't push the students if they cannot answer soon.

If you ask a student a question and she cannot answer, move on to another student or have other students help, but make sure you come back to that student with the same question or another question not too long afterwards, and try to ensure that the question you ask is at the right level for the student—building confidence is very important at this stage. Alternatively, simply encourage the student to say something that will give her a sense of achievement.

VOCABULARY

The words and phrases in this section will be useful throughout the unit. They are not all in the Points Of View section or any other section. They are basic words and phrases that students will need to express themselves during the course of the unit. The purposes of this section are to establish whether the students know these words and can use them, and to give the students a chance to try and make natural sentences with the ones they do not know or cannot use.

There are many ways to teach this section depending on the needs of the students and the style of the teacher. Some teachers will prefer to spend quite a lot of time on this section, and others will prefer to get through it quickly. Some teachers will go straight into the gap-fill exercise, some will get the students to make sentences with the vocabulary, and others will use games or puzzles. Some teachers will do an activity with the words from this section, and others will mix in many words from previous units. If there is time, getting the students to make sentences in fun activities and mixing in other words from previous units are to be strongly recommended.

New words

Whatever style is used, if the students do not know a word/phrase or cannot put it into a sentence, give hints to lead them towards correct answers. If this does not work, make real sentences about yourself, famous people, or subjects the students are interested in—use as much humor as possible—and then invite students to try to make similar sentences. Avoid explanation or translation. Encourage the students to guess the meaning of words/phrases from your sentences, and to consolidate their understanding through trial and error.

It is always best to encourage the students to make sentences that have as much personal meaning for them as possible (see the section on Personalization).

Student-centered approach

If you decide to use a game or a student-centered activity of some kind, it is important for the teacher not to pre-teach before the activity. It is the activity that increases students' desire to know how to use the new words and phrases, and encourages them to ask the teacher for hints or sample sentences. Just go straight into the activity, starting with words you think the students may know, and wait for the activity to motivate the students to ask questions about the words they do not know or cannot use. If they do not do this, it is likely that the activi-

ty is not the right one for the class. Different classes are motivated by different activities.

When students cannot make sentences during an activity, encourage them to ask you for help. It may take time before some of the students ask for your help without hesitation, but that moment is worth planning and waiting for. When students start asking about the things they do not know, it is a sign that their natural curiosity, that may have been suppressed in many years of teacher-centered classes, is beginning to come back. And it is their involvement in the activity that motivates them to risk being curious.

When a student asks about a word she does not know, the teacher makes sample sentences that illustrate the meaning of the word without explaining the meaning. The students then make their own sentences.

Example	*New Word:* Fronkled
Student:	Fronkled! Huh! What does that mean?
Teacher:	Help her.
Other students:	Huh! Please help us!
Teacher:	Well, I'm pretty fronkled after a hard day's work (sigh). I also get real fronkled after going jogging (sigh), and extremely fronkled after teaching you! (sigh). How about you?
Student:	I'm pretty fronkled after studying English.

SOME POSSIBLE VOCABULARY ACTIVITIES

One or more of these activities can be used:

Straightforward approach
The students make sentences with these words and phrases either orally around the class, with or without pair practice first, or in writing.

The Stages of a Unit

Usage

Ask the students to suggest when we use each word/phrase either before or after making a sentence. If there is time, they can first do this in pairs before reporting to the whole class.

Synonyms and definitions

Ask the students to think of synonyms or definitions of some or all of the words/phrases. This will not be easy for some of the words/phrases so it is best to write down selected words/phrases on the board. The students can also work on this in pairs first.

Match the synonym or definition

Give the students synonyms or definitions and have the students guess which synonym/definition goes with each word.

Word association

The students think of other words or ideas they associate with some or all of the words/phrases. This can be done as a brainstorming session with the whole class with or without pair practice first.

Adding more words

The students think of more words/phrases which they associate with the theme of the unit and that could be added to the list. This can also be done with or without pair practice first.

What's the missing word?

Write sentences on the board with a space for one of the words from the list. The students guess what the word is. If possible, write sentences that mean something to you (i.e. not ones about 'John' or 'Mary' but about you or people/things you are genuinely interested in). This is a very gentle activity which can work well with a new class.

Race

In pairs or teams the students race to work out definitions of each of the words in the list.

Timed talk

Students try to talk without hesitation for a fixed amount of time (e.g. two mins) on a word from the list. This can be done as a game where a successful student wins points for her team.

Making corrections

Make incorrect sentences with the words/phrases and have the students work out what the mistakes are. An alternative is to give them a choice of sentences, one of which is correct.

Odd one out

Make groups of words (usually three) and get the students to decide which one is the odd one out and give a reason. It's not necessary to choose words that have an obvious connection.

Questioning

The teacher writes a list of sample questions on the board:

Example: Where can we find a _____?
                Why do some people _____?
                How many times a day do you
                see a _____?
                Who often _____?
                Where do _____ come from?
                + 3 more questions of your choice.

The students are in pairs. One student asks the questions and the other answers, and they then switch roles. The teacher throws out a word from a list—if it is an adjective or adverb, the teacher puts it with a noun or verb, or gets the students to do this if they can.

Make a story

The students try to make a story that connects as many of the words together as possible. This is usually best done in pairs or teams.

Card activities

The students have cards for words/phrases from the present list and from previous units. The words from previous units should be for any words/phrases the students found difficult or needed more practice with, not just the words in the vocabulary sections. Ideally, these cards should be made by each student, but this may or may not be feasible. If not, the teacher should make them and, where possible, each student can have a set.

N.B. It can help students a lot to have these cards even if there are no card activities in the class.

Whether or not students have personal sets, they can play card games such as Snap, Concentration (needs two sets), UNO (with numbers on the cards), or any game the students like. Each time they play a card, or, if this slows down the game too much, each time something special and positive (not a penalty) happens such as winning a trick, they make a sentence with the card they have played.

They can also play board games such as snakes and ladders and turn over the top card from a pile either before throwing the dice or before something special happens such as going up a ladder.

Grid games

Put the words/phrases from the current unit and previous units in grids and play games such as bingo, tic tac toe, tiddleywinks, or throwing games. The students make sentences with the words/phrases either each turn or when something special happens in the game (such as when a student wins bingo she makes a sentence with each word in her winning line).

(a) Bingo

Dictate words that students write down anywhere on a bingo grid, putting one word in each square. Each of these words is also put in a box. The students take turns to draw a word from the box and call it out. A student that completes a line in any direction calls out 'bingo'. A student that gets bingo has to make a sentence with each of the words in the line.

(b) Tic Tac Toe

Write words in each square of a tic tac toe grid either on the board or on pieces of paper for the students to play with in pairs. The most difficult words should be in the center of the grid.

An improvement on the original tic tac toe game is to use a 4x4 or 5x5 grid. The students are in two teams, and take turns to place an O or X in the grid. A team gets a point for getting three Os or Xs in a row, either horizontally, vertically, or diagonally. An O or X later in the game can often be worth two or three points.

(c) Tiddleywinks

Make a tiddleywinks board with a word in each square, and allocate points to each square according to the difficulty of the word. Students flick a counter or coin onto the board and collect points.

Throwing

Use something that sticks to the board, such as a sticky ball, an arrow shot from a bow etc... Write words/phrases in a target on the board. These can be conventional targets, grid games, pictures of animals, or something else that is visually stimulating. When students hit a word, they make a sentence and get points for that word, try to get a line of words etc...

Another kind of throwing game is to play some version of basketball where the students throw a soft ball into a basket, a dice into a box etc... and make a sentence with a word/phrase each time they throw or whenever they succeed.

Ladders

Draw a ladder on the board that has clear stages. The stages used depend on the kinds of students in the class. With some classes, the bottom of the ladder could be things like spiders or cockroaches, and the top an alien. With other students, the ladder could reflect the grades of management in their company.

The students are in teams and take turns to make sentences with words/phrases. They move up one stage of the ladder either after making a sentence (or a certain number of sentences) or after doing some additional task such as throwing a dice and getting a 5 or 6 or throwing a soft ball into a basket.

Board activities

(a) Spaces

Put the students in teams. Think of a sentence

The Stages of a Unit

that includes one of the target words (in a mixed level class, a student with higher English ability can do this) and write it on the board, putting a dash instead of each letter in the sentence. The students take turns to call out a letter. If the letter is in the sentence, the teacher writes down the letter above each dash that corresponds to that letter. After each correct guess, the team can try to guess the sentence.

This is a variation of Hangman, but in fact any scoring system can be used. For example, after guessing the sentence a student can try to throw a dice into a box.

(b) Mixed-up sentences

Make sentences using a few of the words, and then scatter them around the board (or on handouts). Say how many sentences there are. The students try to separate the sentences out from the mass of words.

(c) Telepathy

Write about four sentences on the board. Each sentence contains one of the target words (humorous sentences work best). One student stands in front of the class, secretly chooses a sentence, then closes her eyes and tries to send the sentence to the other students telepathically. The other students close their eyes and try to receive the sentence. The students then say which sentence they chose, and see if it is correct. They then do the same activity in groups, taking turns to send out the sentence, and getting points for receiving it correctly. The teacher gradually changes the sentences, using more of the words.

Gap-fill exercise

The gap-fill exercise below the vocabulary section can either be used for consolidation after the students have done one or more activities with the vocabulary, or it can be used at an earlier stage to assess the students' understanding of the vocabulary. Each student can do the exercise individually, in pairs, or the whole class can work together on finding the possible answers. Even if the students first work by themselves, it is best to bring the class together and ask them to suggest answers.

Please note that more than one of the

words/phrases in the vocabulary section may fit in some of the gaps. This is deliberate. The students need to get used to the idea that English is not mathematics with clear right or wrong answers. If the students are not clear about any of the answers, it may be helpful to practice a few more personalized sentences together.

Finally, ask the students to answer the question below the gap-fill exercise. They can also do this activity individually, in pairs, or as a class. Encourage them to think of people, free time activities, things that happened to them in the past etc… and think of words that would be useful to describe these topics. They may need to use dictionaries to look for new words, or get help from you or the other students.

MIND MAP

Ask the students to look at the mind map in the unit just to get a general idea of how a mind map works, and to get some specific ideas. Then start a mind map on the board using one of the starting points suggested below the map in the book, or another related topic.

Base the board mind map around one of the more confident students. For example write 'Keeping healthy' in the center of the mind map, and invite her to say or write ideas that spring to mind when she thinks of 'Keeping healthy'. Encourage the other students to help her by making suggestions.

If one of the ideas connected to 'Keeping healthy' is 'going to the gym', encourage her to say or write things that spring to mind when she thinks about going to the gym. Either you or she writes these ideas on the board, branching off from 'going to the gym'. After the map is finished, ask the student to talk about 'going to the gym', using the map as a reference point, going through each train of thought, and elaborating on it when possible. All the students then work out their own mind maps, and talk through them with each other in pairs, in groups, or to the class if the class is small.

It is important to remember that mind maps are best used as a way for individual students to organize their own individual thoughts. The class exercise just mentioned is a good starting point which gets the students used to the idea of mind maps, but, as soon as possible, the students should be preparing their maps individually to organize their own personal thoughts.

Mind maps can also form the basis for personal-ized writing either in the lesson or for homework. The students write short essays using their maps as frameworks. Whether or not this is possible will probably depend on the nature of the course, but this kind of writing practice is invaluable in helping the students clarify their thoughts and develop the ability to express themselves in English.

2nd page of a unit: Points Of View

POINTS OF VIEW

General considerations

The students can listen to the discussion on the audio program or read by the teacher or other students, or read the dialogue, or both.

Listening

Using the audio program in class
(a)   If students are taking an intensive course or having a class almost every day, using the audio program regularly can lead to a distinct improvement in students' ability to listen to English.

(b)   If students have only one or two lessons a week and little exposure to English between classes, there is little evidence to suggest that listening to an audio program will make much difference to the students' ability to listen to English, so in these kinds of learning situations it is more important to encourage students to listen to English for a short time every day out of class. It may help if each student has a copy of the audio program with this book, and is encouraged to listen to it in the car, every evening before going to sleep etc...

So, when lessons are infrequent, if the audio program is used in class it is more to provide variety, to stimulate the students' interest, to learn how to focus on particular aspects of the conversation, and to encourage the students to use the audio program at home and give them the confidence to do so, rather than because it is going to make much difference to their listening ability.

(c)   For teachers who are not native speakers, using the audio program in class may give the students exposure to more natural intonation and pronunciation. If the teacher is a native speaker, using the audio program may give the students exposure to a wider variety of pronunciation.

(d)   If the text is easy for the students, it is more challenging for them to listen to the discussion with books closed than to read it. They can then answer comprehension questions or manipulate the language (see below) before looking at the text.

Things to consider
(a)   Listening to an audio program is often a passive classroom activity, and encourages the students to be followers rather than active participants in the class. With motivated classes, this may not matter at all, but with other classes passive activities of this kind can undermine the work we have been doing to get the students to be active learners.

The Stages of a Unit

Using the activities suggested below helps reduce this feeling. However, even when we do many interesting activities, listening to an audio program can easily feel like an activity the teacher wants students to do, rather than something they are emotionally involved in. With some highly motivated classes, it does not matter very much if a lesson feels like a lesson, but with other students this feeling can have a very negative effect on the effectiveness of the class.

(b)   In some situations, particularly in language schools, students may feel that 'listening' is something they can do at home, and they want to spend as much time as possible practicing 'speaking'. This is particularly the case if they have classes only once or twice a week.

Reading

The students can either read the dialogue after listening to it, or they can read it instead of listening to it. Some teachers believe that silent reading is important, and others believe it is important for students to practice reading aloud so the teacher can help them improve their intonation and pronunciation. Which is right? Perhaps it partly depends on what the students want to do, and it certainly depends on whether they need to practice reading aloud and improve their pronunciation.

But there is a more fundamental issue. Whatever the method, the key question is 'Are the students involved in what they are doing?' If they regard reading as a rather flat classroom activity, then get it over with as quickly as possible, or interrupt it and bring it alive with some of the activities suggested below.

It can also help to encourage students to read with dramatic intonation. For example, if students take the roles of the characters, you could ask one student to read very sadly, and another to read angrily. Another similar method is to get the students to read the dialogue to each other in pairs, and while they are reading, hold up adverb cards (or even better, have a student do this) such as 'fast', 'slowly', 'romantically', 'quietly', 'loudly',

'angrily' etc... The students read with the emotion written on the card or called out by you or a student. Keep changing the cards. The whole point is to get some emotion into the activity. But, of course, with many classes this may not be necessary, or the students may be too self-conscious and not ready to do this kind of thing.

Activities

It can help a lot to have activities before, during, and after listening to or reading the discussion. These activities draw the students into the discussion or the particular language in this section, make it more alive and relevant, and help the students internalize the patterns more deeply so they can use them actively. The activities marked * are in each of the 'listening/reading worksheets' in this Teacher's Book. The other activities are alternatives:

Before listening or reading

Warm-up questions *
Ask the students questions which are directly connected with the discussion in this section, or put them into pairs and encourage them to answer each question. An alternative is for them to first write down their answers and then discuss each other's answers in pairs.

Anticipation gap-fill *
The students are given sentences from the discussion with one or more words missing. They try and guess what the words might be before listening to or reading the discussion. While they are reading or listening, they can see whether they were correct or not.

Natural conversation
Chat with the students about the topic. During this natural conversation, either ask questions using patterns in the text, or help them express what they want to say using some of the words or patterns in the text. Try to make this as natural as possible.

Pre-reading/listening questions
Ask the students questions for the students to

answer while reading or listening to the text. It is usually best to write these questions on the board unless the text is quite easy for the students.

Characters

Tell the students the topic of the discussion and who is taking part, and ask them what they expect each character to think. This works better later in the book when the students have gotten to know the characters.

Mixing things up

Put sentences from the discussion into word puzzles on the board for the students to try and solve with their books closed.

(a) For example (mixing letters)
TOMOKO HSNTIK TI UDWLO EB CUMH ARFSE
CARLOS NTKISH HESS EGBNI AINVTEGE

(b) For example (mixing words)
safer Tomoko much be would it thinks
being Carlos she's negative thinks

The students then see if they were right when they listen to or read the discussion.

Clouds

Put words in one or more clouds on the board. One way to select the words is to choose the key words in a character's opinion. The students then try and see how the words could be combined.
For example:

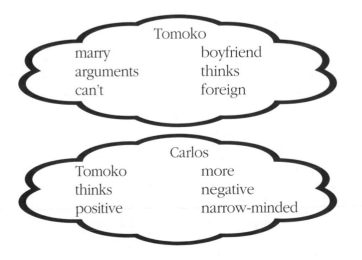

Game

Choose a mixture of easy and difficult words or patterns from the discussion and play a game such as one of those suggested in the vocabulary section.

While listening or reading

*Listening/reading for gist ***

Dictate or write questions for the students to try and answer while listening or reading. These questions should not be about specific points in the text, but should be more general and elicit their general impressions.

*Noticing words ***

Give the students a list of words or expressions, and ask them to circle the ones they hear or see.

*Reading search ***

Have the students search the text for words from definitions, synonyms, words which collocate with those in the text, words beginning with a certain letter etc...

Reading race

Say a word and have the students race to find it. The winning student/team then puts the word into one or more different sentences.

Manipulating language

The students first listen to and/or read the whole discussion, and then listen or read again in short sections. Encourage them to manipulate the language during these pauses. Here are some techniques:

(a) Rephrasing

See if the students can suggest other ways of expressing an idea in the discussion. Some of the ways this can be done are:

Give a starting prompt:
Sentence in text: I'm sure we'd have arguments.
Prompts from teacher: certain
                                        no doubt

The Stages of a Unit

Ask for alternative words/phrases

Sentence in text:	It'd be better if I marry somebody who's more similar to me in character.
Teacher:	Change 'more similar to'.
Students:	It'd be better if she marries somebody who's more like her.
	It'd be better if she marries somebody who's less different from her.
	It'd be better if she marries somebody who shares more of her values.

It may be necessary to give hints and prompts to elicit these alternative expressions.

(b) Personalization

Have the students make personalized sentences using the patterns in the text (see the section on Personalization). The patterns in the text have been selected for their transferability so personalization is likely to be an effective way to manipulate the language in the text.

A variation on this is for the students to read or listen to sections of the discussion and immediately give their opinions. This can either be done after first reading or listening to the whole discussion all the way through, or before this happens. It mainly depends on the level of the students and whether you want to build confidence or challenge the students.

(c) Synonyms/word association

See if the students can think of synonyms for words in the text or ask them to think of other words they associate with a word in the text.

(d) Collocations

See if the students can suggest other words that collocate with words or phrases in the text (see the Collocation Sets section).

(e) Register

See if the students can suggest how to make an expression more or less polite.

(f) Comprehension personalization in chains

See below for a full explanation. These chains can be set up during pauses in the text so as to immediately make the patterns relevant and personal.

After listening or reading

General questions *

The students write or ask each other general questions on the text.

It is best to avoid questions that only get the students to give short answers or where they have a 50% chance of getting the correct answer. Some examples are:

Question:	Is Tomoko sure they'd have arguments?
Student:	Yes.
Question:	Tomoko is sure they'd have arguments. True or false?
Student:	True.

These methods tell us very little about whether the students have understood.

Correct these statements *

The students correct the false statements in the worksheets.

Alternatively, make correct and incorrect statements from the text and have the students correct you when you make mistakes. One way to do this is to close the book or appear to only half listen to the audio program, and pretend you have forgotten much of what was said in the discussion, or genuinely forget—the more genuine your mistakes sound to the students, the more likely it will be that they will speak out and correct you. It is best to use as much humor as possible.

It is worth noting that it is generally good to be a fallible teacher and make mistakes to get the students to speak out more. It is natural for any of us to be intimidated in a conversation if we feel the other person knows much more than us, and this is how most students feel about their teachers. Looked at from this point of view, it is quite natural that so many students do not speak out spontaneously in class but happily do so when they are with their friends. Being a fallible teacher is one way to deal with this problem.

Teacher:	Now what was it Tomoko said? I think she said she was sure they'd have a lot of children.
Student(s):	No.
Teacher:	What's the matter?
Student(s):	She's sure they'd have arguments.
Teacher:	Are you sure?
Student(s):	Yes!
Teacher:	I must have a bad memory. And Tomoko thinks she can't help ... etc…

It can be a lot of fun to be the absent-minded teacher. It is a role you can maintain for much of the lesson, and it encourages a lot more activity and spontaneity even from quite shy classes.

The students can also do the same thing in pairs. One student pretending to be very absent minded, and the other student correcting her.

Comprehension/personalization questions *

The students can write answers or ask each other the questions in the worksheets, or they can practice in chains around the class. Here are some examples of chains:

(a) Basic technique

Teacher:	What is Tomoko sure about?
Student 1:	She's sure they'll have arguments if she marries her boyfriend.
Teacher:	You ... (gestures for the student to ask another student)
Student 1:	What are you sure about?
Student 2:	I'm sure I'll miss my bus if this lesson doesn't finish soon.

You can just leave it at that, or the students can ask each other in a chain around the class.

(b) Starting from a negative answer

Teacher:	Is she sure they'll have a lot of children?

Student 1:	No, she isn't.
Teacher:	What ...? (gestures for student 1 to ask student 2)
Student 1:	What is she sure about?
Student 2:	She's sure they'll have a lot of arguments.
Teacher:	You? (gestures for student 2 to ask student 3)
Student 2:	What are you sure about?
Student 3:	I'm sure I'll miss my bus if this lesson doesn't finish soon.

Once the students have got used to the technique, they can ask the initial question. They ask questions which are absurd or obviously not true (humor works best), so as to elicit a negative answer.

Pair checking

One student looks at the text and asks the other student questions about it. They then reverse roles. If the students are used to the kind of practice in the Comprehension/personalization section above, they can follow each answer with a personalized example. For example:

Student 1:	What is Tomoko sure about?
Student 2:	She's sure they'd have arguments if they get married.
Student 1:	What are you sure about?
Student 2:	I'm sure I'll miss my bus if this lesson doesn't finish soon.

Remembering

Get the students to close their books and see how much they can remember about what each of the characters said. The idea is to focus on meaning not on the exact language used.

One variation on this is for a student from one team to speak for one minute, and then to quickly point to a student from another team to continue speaking. If a student, with help from her team, stops talking or runs out of things to say, the team loses.

Summarizing/interviewing

Ask the students to summarize the arguments of one or more of the characters. They can do this as

The Stages of a Unit

a class—helping each other—or individually. They can also summarize in pairs.

A way of doing the same kind of thing in a more involved and imaginative way is for one student in a pair to be a TV interviewer or newspaper reporter and the other student to be one of the characters in the story. They can reverse roles, with the student who was the interviewer becoming the other character in the discussion. The interviewers can ask questions directly related to the text or, if the students are ready for this, they can get into their roles more and take the interviews in any directions they like.

3rd page of a unit: Practice and Discussion

PERSONALIZATION

Personalization is used extensively at every stage of a unit and this section is a way to consolidate the students' ability to personalize some of the patterns encountered in the previous section. It is also a stepping stone between the text and the discussion at the bottom of the page.

The students practice the sentences either in pairs or around the class. They should be encouraged to give any examples that are true for them. Each student should have a chance to answer every question. It is important for them to practice orally at this stage, and they should not be restricted by the theme of the unit or the discussion in the text.

Some students will give simple answers and others will be more ambitious. At this stage of the lesson, it is best to encourage students to be as ambitious as they can, but it is important to know their limit and not push them too far.

It may take practice before all the students are comfortable with this kind of activity—some of the sentences require quite a lot of imagination. Give prompts, hints and examples about yourself if necessary, but back away as the students get the idea.

The questions in this section are only a starting point. If you have noticed any patterns the students seem to have difficulty with either in this unit or in previous units, you can add them to this section either by writing extra questions on the board or allocating more questions individually.

It is best to keep a notebook for jotting down patterns the students find difficult. In many situations it may be best to make a mental note of a problem and write it down during a natural break rather than interrupt the flow of an activity or discussion. This can also be done at other stages of a lesson.

Definition

The word 'personalization' has been used a number of times so far. When students personalize words or structures, this generally means they use these words and structures in sentences about themselves.

Example: I'm sure I'll miss my bus.

Rather than fictional people:

Example: John (or Mary) is sure he'll miss his bus.

It can also mean the students make sentences about their family, friends, neighborhood, country, books/movies they like, topics of conversation that get them excited etc...

The emotional dimension of 'personalization' is particularly important. Students should be encouraged to talk or write about subjects they have a genuine feeling about. If it is not important to a student whether her brother likes swimming, then to say 'My brother likes swimming' is not really a personalized sentence.

One of our major roles as teachers is to discover

the world in which our students really live. We can then encourage and prompt them to give as many examples as possible from this world.

To find out what is important for our students, it may help to give a questionnaire to a new class.

The kind of questions asked will depend on the age and level of the students, but here is an example of what can be done. It is sometimes best to ask students to write in their native language—this may give you more useful information.

Questionnaire

1. Family
Give information about each member of your family (name, age, occupation), and write a few sentences about each of them.

2. Friends
Give information about two or three of your best friends, and write a few sentences about each of them.

3. Books
Name the two books you like best, and say why you like them.
Name one book you don't like and say why.

4. Movies
Name the two movies you like best, and say why you like them.
Name one movie you don't like and say why.

5. Sport
Name your favorite sport and say why you like it.
Name a sport you don't like and say why.

6. Sundays
Name two things you like to do on Sundays and say why.
Name one thing you don't like to do on Sundays and say why.

7. Topics
Name one topic you enjoy talking about and say why.
Name one topic you don't enjoy talking about and say why.

8. Respect
Name two people you respect and say why.
Name one person you don't respect and say why.

9. Work
Name one job you would like to do in future and say why.
Name one job you wouldn't like to do and say why.

10. Ambitions
Name two things (not work) you would like to do in future and say why.
Name one thing you wouldn't want to do in future and say why.

11. Routine
Name two things you have to do almost every day that you don't like.
Name two things you have to do almost every day that you like very much.

12. Home
Do you like your house/apartment? Say why.
Where would you ideally like to live? Why?

The Stages of a Unit

You can get a lot of information from a questionnaire like this. It is not just the facts. It is often what is implied that is just as important as the opinions themselves.

Examples:

If a student says she respects somebody because he's tall and generous, then there's a good chance the constructs 'tall-short' and 'mean-generous' may be important for that student.

If a student says the person he most respects is his mother and the thing he most likes doing is cooking dinner, you can begin to get a better picture of at least one of the worlds that is important for him, and can put examples into that world.

This is only a starting point. As you get to know the students better, you will modify and often completely change your ideas about what's important for them. It can take some time before we can really get into the world of each of our students and, just as importantly, for them to get into our world, but whether we can achieve this or not will often dictate the success or failure of our classes. The questionnaire is just an initial step on the road to understanding, which, of course, never ends.

JOKES

(also applies to the jokes on the other pages)

Humor is an essential part of any lesson for so many reasons. It motivates and increases the students' emotional involvement in the lesson. Emotion is a central part of learning, and plays an even more important role in increasing retention. So often, students remember a language point because they associate it with an enjoyable or humorous situation. Having jokes on a page also draws students into the material by making it much more approachable. A page that feels like 'studying' is so often pushed aside, both during the lesson and at home after the lesson.

Using the jokes in class
STEP 1
Ask the students questions either to help them understand the jokes or to check they understand the language. For example, if the joke depends on a pun, ask them to guess the two meanings of the key word.

Example: "Are you decisive?"
                 "Yes and no."

Teacher: Is he decisive?
              How do you know?
              How often is he decisive?

STEP 2
Have the students make personalized sentences (see the section on personalization) using the key words/phrases in the joke dialogue. Either all the students or a few individual students can do this orally, or they can all try to write personalized sentences.

Example: In what kinds of situations do you tend to be decisive? (ask each other)
         In what kinds of situations do you tend to be indecisive? (ask each other)
         Who do you think can be too decisive? (ask each other)
         Who irritates you when they are indecisive? (ask each other)

DISCUSSION

This section is what the previous sections have been leading up to. By now, the students should, at least potentially, have the tools to discuss the questions in this section and others like them. They should now be given free rein to speak and speak and speak, and it is often a good idea to add more discussion questions to the ones in the book. They can do this as a class or in pairs. It depends on the number of students and whether they all speak out or not. Larger classes or classes that include students that don't speak out a lot should do these discussion questions in pairs.

In each unit, there are three Discussion Strategies for the students to use during the discussions. It is best to write these on the board before the discussion starts. It may also help to write expressions from previous units that you would like the students to use, and any key vocabulary or expressions from the current unit or previous units you would like the students to practice.

To get the maximum benefit from this discussion time, it is necessary to be careful about the following points:

Domination by individual students

One of the main problems in many classes is that discussions are dominated by one or two students. It is essential to do everything possible to prevent this from happening, otherwise some of the other students can easily lose confidence or speak out much less than they would if the dominant students were not there. The most subtle way is simply to put all the students in pairs and make sure a dominant student is not talking with a student that can be intimidated. Another way is to direct questions to individuals that aren't participating as much.

Partiality

Another problem is that we may identify more with students that speak out a lot or have opinions that are close to our own, and this can intimidate other students or make them feel excluded. This is often subtle. The students that aren't included may not say anything. They may just become quieter, more polite, or find an excuse for not attending the class. To avoid this, we need to step back and take a long professional look at the role we are playing in the class.

Teacher domination

A third problem is that we may dominate discussions, even when it seems we are hardly speaking. It is very likely that we will win any discussion. We may think this is because our argument is wonderful and everybody is agreeing with us, but it may simply be because we haven't really given enough openings for students to express their real opinions, or encouraged them to say things that are difficult to express in English. Students do often

want to know what we think, and giving our opinion is an important part of making human contact with the students. It is good if students can get into our world as much as we get into theirs. However, there are really only three occasions on which we should give our opinions:

(1) When the students aren't speaking a lot or only making superficial comments, we may need to provoke or play devil's advocate so as to add some spice to the discussions. If students are only saying superficial things, they will tend to use easy and familiar patterns. If students are worked up and trying to say something important to them, it is much more likely that they will search for new ways of saying things and hopefully find that using some of the words and structures introduced earlier in the unit can help them express themselves.

(2) After the students have been given a lot of chances to express themselves.

(3) When students ask us genuine questions. This is the most difficult one. We want to answer their questions, but we mustn't do so too convincingly otherwise we'll have too big an influence on the subsequent discussion, and we must put the ball back in their court as soon as possible. A brief, genuine answer followed by a return question is often the best policy.

Students don't use new words and structures

The students may talk a lot, but not try to use the words and structures they have been learning in the previous stages of the unit. Their English ability may not really be moving forward very much. This is usually because one of the previous sections of the unit has not been done thoroughly enough. This does not mean that every activity suggested so far has to be done in every class—it depends very much on the class and time avail-

The Stages of a Unit

able—but if students are not using the target language during the discussions, it is worth looking back at the previous stages of the unit and thinking about which section might need to be emphasized more. It is also important to ask whether the students have been emotionally involved enough in the previous stages of the unit—without this emotional dimension to learning, the new language is less likely to be used spontaneously in the discussions.

With some classes, an added incentive is for students to award themselves points for including particular words and structures in their discussions. Before the discussion begins, write the words and structures in a list on the board with points next to each of them. You can award more points for words/structures that are more difficult or ones you particularly want the students to practice. This list should include words/structures from earlier units, and ones that are not in the book but the students have had difficulty with.

4th page of a unit: Activities

FOLLOW-UP QUESTIONS

These are usually quick activities done in pairs. However, if necessary, start by asking quick questions around the class and immediately follow up each answer with another question:

For example: (unit 1)

Teacher:	What do you think is one of your good points?
Student 1:	I think I'm positive?
Teacher:	Can you think of a situation where you weren't positive?

Once the students have been loosened up, go straight into the activity.

Reporting back

It often helps if individual pairs report back to the rest of the class. One student can report back on what the other student has said or they can demonstrate a sample dialogue. If students know this may happen, they are likely to concentrate harder during the pair work activity. Avoid putting students in a situation where they are likely to fail. Whatever you ask the students to report should be something they are capable of reporting with some help from you.

ROLE PLAYS

These activities can also be done fairly quickly. If necessary, help one pair demonstrate each activity to the rest of the students. If they are not sitting in a place where the other students can see what's going on, the pair can be brought out to the front of the class. It is important not to get the model pair to model a precise dialogue you want the students to practice or even to go too far into any kind of practice. The model pair should do just enough to get the others started and give them a general idea of what they could do.

Many of the role plays give students the option of being themselves or a famous person. In these cases, each student chooses who they will be and tells the other student in their pair. They then each write down questions they would like to ask each other. First one student plays the role of asking questions, and then the other.

Even in those role plays where there are no reporters, each student should have some time to prepare things to say and questions to ask. They then practice the role play, and may give a demonstration in front of the other students.

SITUATIONS

In this section, the students cover a wide range

of everyday situations, and learn and practice everyday language patterns that intermediate students may not be familiar with or be able to use. The example patterns given in the book are just a starting point. Every teacher has their own favorite everyday expressions and these should be introduced as well, bearing in mind that we can never be sure where our students will use their English in the future, so the expressions should preferably be ones they can use all over the world.

The situations and suggested patterns in these sections are deliberately a little dramatic and sometimes humorous. The emphasis is on getting the students emotionally involved in what they are doing. At the same time, we need to realize that many of our students may be intimidated by elaborate role plays and hesitate to use exaggerated gestures. The situations in this book have been designed to be achievable by most classes and in most cultures.

STEP 1

Lead into each situation with a brief warm-up activity such as one of the following:

(a) Brainstorming

Brainstorm using the questions in the student's book or other similar questions. You can do this with the whole class, or have the students brainstorm in pairs and then report their ideas to you. Sometimes the students will want to look at the book for ideas. Let them do this. It means they are choosing to open the book and study the examples there, and this is the kind of attitude we want to encourage.

Target situation: You are a psychiatrist. Try to advise Student B.

Teacher: Think of reasons somebody might have to go to a psychiatrist.

Students: They've been working hard.
Their girl/boyfriend has just left them.
They are always depressed.
They are thinking of killing themselves.

(write down each pattern on the board)

Add touches to the expressions the students suggest to make them more natural.

Student A: They've been working hard..

Teacher: How do we say somebody's been working too hard?

Student B: They've been working much too hard.

Teacher: Or … They've been ov…

Student C: They've been overworking.

(b) Questioning

Isolate some of the target patterns you would like the students to focus on and put them in questions to the students.

Target pattern: … like this/like that.

Teacher: How are you feeling?

Student A: I have a cold.

Teacher: How long have you been feeling like this?
etc…

After throwing out a few questions in this way, write the framework of the patterns on the board, and have the students try to use them in pairs.

(c) Personalized sentences

Write down target patterns on the board or throw them out to the class one at a time. The students make personalized sentences in writing or orally as a class or in pairs.

Example: I've tried everything …
I'm madly in love with …

The Stages of a Unit

(d) Puzzles

Put some of the target patterns into a puzzle.

Target patterns:	How often does that happen? I can't live without her. Have you tried not meeting him?

Scatter the words from these three sentences all over the board. If appropriate, put them inside a cloud or simple picture. The students try to separate out the three sentences.

(e) Mini-situations

Act out a mini-situation to lead into a more complex situation.

Target situation:	Giving advice
Teacher:	(tell the students imaginary problems) My dog is sick. I don't know what to do.
Students:	(teacher helps students say these kinds of expressions) What exactly is the matter? Why don't you take him/her to a clinic?

STEP 2

The students do the activity in the book. There are many ways of doing this, and most teachers will have their own ways of dealing with these kinds of situations. Here are some possibilities:

(a) Model pair

With a large class, bring a pair of students out to the front of the class. With a small class, the pair you choose can stay in their seats. Say which student is A and which student is B, either outline their role to them or have them read through their roles, and go straight into the situation and see what happens.

Encourage the students to try, and help them to improve the expressions they use, wherever possible leading them towards the patterns in the book or other patterns you think are important. The important thing is to encourage them to get into the role and just speak.

The model pair shouldn't demonstrate for too long, and they certainly shouldn't practice a dialogue for the other students to copy exactly. The idea is to continue long enough for the other students to understand what they need to do, but not longer than this.

Then all the students do the activity in pairs with books open, using the sample patterns to help them. Walk around the class, encouraging the students to speak out and say what they want to say rather than copy what the model students said.

(b) Mime

Either you mime the roles of both A and B, or use a model pair helping them with each mime until they get the idea. Either you or the students mime a stage of the situation and encourage the other students to suggest what to say.

Example:	One student walks into a psychiatrist's office, opening the door. The psychiatrist gestures for the student to lie down. (gesture to ask the rest of the class what the psychiatrist might say) etc...

Either the class suggest a conversation which the students in front of the class mime, or they mime a situation, and the class suggest what they may say, or a combination of the two.

After going through a situation like this, do it again completely silently—the students to do all the talking. One way is to divide the class into two teams, one team work together to play A's role, and the other team play B's role.

The students then do the activity in pairs with books open.

(c) Working alone

Divide the class into pairs or groups. Each pair/group looks at the situation in the book and tries to work out what to do. Then ask some pairs or groups to demonstrate the dialogue they have come up with. The idea is to let the students try and understand and think through what to do by themselves. With some classes, it can be fun to make the demonstrations into a contest.

STEP 3

For some classes, there may be no time, or it may be unnecessary, to do more with these situations. However, with other classes it would be best to extend and widen the patterns practiced so far. Here are some ideas for what can be done:

(a) Related situations

The students search for what to say in situations that are somehow related to the one in the book.

Sample situation: Give advice to famous people who have problems, either real or imaginary.

Teacher: Think of famous people and the problems they might have.

Students: (pairs of students choose a famous person, imagine his or her problems, and list possible advice a psychiatrist might give)

Some or all of the pairs can then act out a scene where one of them is the famous person and the other is a psychiatrist giving advice.

(b) Extension of structures

Write key patterns on the board. These can be the patterns from the book or other patterns that have come out of the previous practice.

Ask the students to make other sentences using these patterns, sometimes providing hints by suggesting other kinds of situations in which they can be used. Alternatively, put the students in pairs, and give them a list of situations to use each pattern in.

5th page of a unit: Further Activities

COLLOCATION SETS

Whenever our students learn new words, it is important for them to learn the other words these words usually combine with. Many combinations of words are possible but some pairs of words occur together very frequently. Knowing the most frequent collocations of a word can help make a student's English a lot more natural.

In this section, there are some common collocations of words related to the theme of the unit. Some example sentences are given, and the aim is for the students to make sentences using the other collocations. They can do this individually, in pairs or as a class.

If the students make mistakes, give some examples, preferably personalized sentences or sentences about subjects that will arouse their interest.

After listening to your examples, they can try again to make their own sentences.

To consolidate their understanding, it can help a lot to do one of the fun activities mentioned in the Vocabulary section. For example, pairs of words that collocate from the current unit and previous units could be put in a tic tac toe grid on the board and the students either play the game in a straightforward way or throw or shoot something at the squares on the board in order to put an O or X in that square. Whenever they choose or hit a square, they make a sentence with the word combination in that square.

SPEECHES

The aim of this section is to give students more confidence and practice in speaking in front of oth-

The Stages of a Unit

ers, either formally or informally, and in helping them to present well-ordered arguments.

Either use the topics suggested, other topics you think are appropriate for a particular class, or any topic related to the theme of the unit that is chosen by each student. This last method can be particularly motivating for some classes.

Students should be given time to prepare their speeches. If necessary, brainstorm the topic with the class before the students start to prepare. Each student then makes a speech, the length of which depends on the number of students in the class and the time available.

Some teachers prefer to allocate a fixed time in each lesson for selected students to make short speeches they have prepared before the lesson. This can also work well.

Questioning

It can be a good idea to have a short question time after a speech, with other students directing questions to the person who made the speech. If students don't ask very probing questions, tell individual students they are newspaper reporters or TV interviewers, and ask them to write down questions while they are listening to the speech. The students then ask these questions, in their role as reporters/interviewers, after the speech.

Interruption game

Each student prepares a speech. Set an alarm without telling the students what time it is set for. One student starts to make her speech. A student can interrupt whenever another student pauses. The student that is talking when the alarm goes off gets a point.

Pauses

Students have to speak for as long as possible. If they pause, they must use a natural pause strategy. If they pause without doing this, their time is finished. The student who speaks the longest is the winner. A variation of this is to allow other students to ask questions to try and throw the student out of her stride.

Example pause strategies:
> repeating the previous statement
> rhetorical questions
> Well ...
> uh ...
> It's like this ...
> You know what I mean ...
> You see ...
> etc...

EXTRA EXPRESSIONS

There is some debate about whether students should learn idioms or not. There is research that seems to show that we hardly ever use many of the idioms that students tend to learn. Of course it depends on the idiom. There are many that we use a lot.

At the same time, it is clear that a lot of students like to learn idioms. A lot of intermediate level students have become tired of learning basic structures, or feel they know them, and grab at idioms as signs of tangible new things they can add to their knowledge. Idioms also can be a lot of fun.

Of course, it depends what we mean by an idiom. Every section of a unit in this book is full of idiomatic expressions, but the expressions in the Extra Expressions section tend to be idiomatic phrases that can be isolated out as individual bits of knowledge. They are there for extra stimulation, and because no intermediate course is really complete without them. They will be appropriate for some classes but not for others, which is why they are on the Further Activities page.

How to introduce them

First see if any of the students can make a sentence with one of the expressions. If they cannot, make some natural (and preferably humorous) sentences yourself until the students get the idea. They can then make their own sentences.

After going through each expression, put the students into pairs, and ask them to try and work out mini-dialogues with each expression. There is an example dialogue in the book to help the students. When they have had time to do this, have sample pairs demonstrate their dialogues to the rest of the class.

The students should finish by writing down sample sentences or dialogues either on flip cards (see the Vocabulary section) or in a special section of a file or note book.

6th page of a unit: Consolidation & Recycling

The activities in this section consolidate what has been learned in the rest of the unit and mix it with language from previous units. They can be used in class or done at home. Doing these activities will make a significant difference to how deeply the students retain words and structures.

It helps if the students do the written exercises except for the crossword on a computer or in a special notebook or file so they can keep a clear record of their progress. If they use computers, encourage them to use software that underlines mistakes or questionable grammar. This helps them reflect more on what they are writing.

BUILDING VOCABULARY

Just give the students the crosswords and see what happens. If you notice many students are having trouble with the same clue, give some hints or prompts to help.

Students can do the crosswords individually, in pairs or in groups. If they are not difficult for the students, it is better for them to be done individually. The answers to the clues come from the current unit or previous units.

FOCUSING ON COLLOCATIONS

The students put each pair of words into a separate sentence, preferably one that is meaningful. The collocation pairs in this section are from the current unit and the previous units.

Correcting written sentences

If a mistake is important, it is often better to indicate where the mistake is in the sentence by underlining the part that is wrong, and, if necessary, give some hint such as the starting word of a better pattern. This can be done in individual students' notebooks or on the board if you feel all the students will benefit from analyzing the mistake (it is not necessary to say which student made the mistake), and then ask students to suggest how to correct the mistake. This also applies when the students have not actually made a mistake but need to improve the style of a sentence.

Example:
Student's sentence:
> Doing overtime has no connection with my tiredness.

Write   'There is ...' on the board.

This might elicit the sentence (maybe with your help):
> There is no connection between my tiredness and having to do overtime.

Cross out 'having' and write '... whether ...'.
The aim is to elicit the sentence:
> There is no connection between my tiredness and whether I do overtime.

Avoid making any student feel bad by their sentence being analyzed and manipulated in this way. If possible, it is best to avoid making it obvious who made the mistake. It may also sometimes be better to change the original sentence a little or make a different model sentence that contains the

The Stages of a Unit

same kind of mistake.

The students can then practice writing sentences that include the pattern you elicited.

WRITING OPINIONS

The students write paragraphs or short essays about each of the topics. Assign a minimum and maximum number of words, if necessary.

To make the activity more fun, students can be given points for including words and structures from a list that they manage to include in the paragraph. Some words/structures can be worth more points than others. You can identify words/structures they have been finding difficult and put them in the list.

If the students find paragraph writing difficult, it may be necessary to brainstorm ideas and arguments before they try and write. One way to do this is to get students to think of any ideas related to the topic and then extend these ideas through a kind of map—starting from one idea and drawing a line to another idea.

For example, you could write 'ideal friends' in a circle in the middle of the board or at the top of the board and ask the students to say anything they associate with this. They may say things like 'always kind', 'helping each other', 'having fun', 'traveling together' etc… You then write these down in circles leading off from the first circle. You then do the same for each of these patterns by asking, 'What do you connect with "having fun"?'. After a while, the students may begin to get ideas about how they could structure their essays.

Correction and rewriting

Correction can be done in the same way as in the Focusing On Collocations section. It can also help a lot if the students rewrite their essays after becoming aware of their mistakes and of how they can improve the style.

REFLECTION

Encourage the students to answer the questions either in class or by writing their answers down and giving them to you. This can be very useful feedback. It is often a good idea to extend the list of questions, so that the students are filling in a short questionnaire at the end of each unit.

It also makes a big difference if the students reflect on the words and structures they found difficult in the unit, and write each of them on separate cards, perhaps with a sample sentence to show their usage. The students can build up this collection of cards and look through them as regularly as possible.

A Final Word

To provide a complete course for your students, you can help them widen their skills by encouraging the following:

Journals

The students keep a diary or notebook and write down anything they like in it. One idea is for students to keep this journal beside their bed, and for them to write down anything that occurs to them just before they sleep. They can write down what they have done that day, what they are think-

ing about … in fact, anything they like.

Whether the students keep a journal, and whether they write or not should be up to them. We can actively encourage them to keep the journal, but it defeats the point if we make it obligatory. We also should not correct very much, if at all, unless a student obviously wants us to.

Extra reading

Encourage the students to read about anything they like. If they are interested in sport, they should read about sport. The more they enjoy what they read, the more reading they will do. They should not look up every word in a dictionary. They should read for content. To maximize the effectiveness of this approach, the level of the material is very important. Recommend graded readers or magazines if appropriate.

Extra listening

Encourage the students to watch TV or listen to radio English language teaching programs if you think they are good and of the right level. You can also introduce them to tapes or listening courses they can use at home. Always be careful about level. Students can sometimes lose a lot of confidence and motivation by watching or listening to TV/radio shows that are too difficult, especially in an environment where they don't generally have much natural exposure to English in their daily lives.

An alternative, that often works very well, is to encourage students to bring small tape recorders to each lesson. They can then listen to the lesson again in their car, at home etc.... This is particularly effective if the students don't have many lessons each week.

DEALING WITH MISTAKES

Don't worry too much about correcting mistakes in the early stages of a unit, though it is always good to make a note of these mistakes so you can deal with them later. In fact, it is best to build up a written list of key mistakes, and to address these problems systematically later in the same lesson or a subsequent lesson. Over a period of time, you can build up a list of the typical language points that your students have trouble with, and keep on coming back to these points.

At the moment the mistake is made, it can help a lot to correct the mistake in a natural way, and then move on without dwelling on the point.

Example:
Student:	Almost of us still live with our parents.
Teacher:	Really! Almost all of you live with your parents. That's surprising!

In this case, the teacher has noticed that 'almost' is being used as a quantity instead of qualifying the quantity, but she does not explain this or make a big point of it. She introduces the correct use of 'almost' in a natural way, and makes a mental note of the problem. At a natural break, she writes down the problem in a book she keeps for this purpose, and comes back to the problem later in the lesson, like this:

Example:
Student:	(reading) I can't help the way I feel.
Teacher:	How about you?
Student:	Yes, of course I can't help feeling the way I do.
Teacher:	Always?
Student:	Well ...
Teacher:	(helps) Almost.
Student:	... almost always. I suppose I can sometimes look carefully at the reasons for my feeling, and try and change it.

Other opportunities to introduce 'almost' come in the Personalization and Focusing On Collocations sections, where the teacher simply adds the structure 'Almost all ...' as a prompt for students to make sentences with. In fact, all key mistakes the students have made in the lesson, and some from previous lessons, can be added as prompts in these sections.

To be honest, a mistake such as the 'almost' problem above can be dealt with in almost any later section of the unit—during discussion, situational practice, written exercises etc...

Sections

1. Attitudes

POINTS OF VIEW: I could never marry a foreigner.

Before listening or reading

A. Warm-up questions:

1. If you fell in love with a foreigner how hard would you try to marry him/her?

_____

2. What's a good way to make your mood more positive?

_____

3. Where would you like to go to experience a more international environment?

_____

B. Anticipation gap-fill:

1. I'm sure we'd have arguments all the _____.

2. The sad thing is it will probably come _____.

3. I can't _____ the way I feel.

4. I think you need to take a close _____ at the reasons for your attitudes.

While listening or reading

Tomoko is the first and third speaker. Carlos is the second and fourth speaker.

C. Listening/reading for gist:

1. Who do you think is more positive, Tomoko or Carlos? _____

2. Who do you think is more pessimistic, Tomoko or Carlos? _____

3. Who do you think is more international, Tomoko or Carlos? _____

D. Noticing words: *(circle the words you hear/see)*

attitude	decisive	way	paranoid
communicate	experience	prejudice	tolerant
easygoing	similar	impossible	negative

E. Reading search:

1. How many words begin with 'p'? _____

2. Find something that means 'I can't do anything about'. _____

3. Find the opposite of 'different from'. _____

4. Find two words that collocate with 'understand'. _____

5. Find a word that goes with 'environment'. _____

After listening or reading

F. General questions:

1. What is Tomoko sure about?

_____

2. What can't Tomoko change?

_____

3. Where does Carlos think Tomoko could go?

_____

G. Correct these statements:

1. Tomoko wishes she could find a way to leave her boyfriend.

_____

2. Carlos thinks Tomoko should go into her marriage with an easygoing attitude.

_____

3. Carlos thinks Tomoko should take a close look at his bicycle.

_____

H. Comprehension/personalization questions:

1. What seems impossible for Tomoko?

_____

2. What seems impossible for you?

_____

3. What would make Tomoko's parents happier?

_____

4. What would make your family happier?

_____

5. What can Tomoko change if she really wants to?

_____

6. What can you change if you really want to?

_____

2. Money

POINTS OF VIEW: Money makes us greedy.

Before listening or reading

A. Warm-up questions:

1. What effects does money often have on people?

_____

2. List three reasons why people work hard.

_____

3. In which ways are you greedy?

_____

B. Anticipation gap-fill:

1. I think we should all get _____ the same amount of money.

2. Money is an incentive to _____.

3. They believe in the social _____ of what they are doing.

4. But you're missing the _____.

While listening or reading

Jin-Sook is the first and third speaker. Nazim is the second and fourth speaker.

C. Listening/reading for gist:

1. Who thinks we should all get the same amount of money? _____

2. Who believes there are many incentives to work?   _____

3. Who thinks we need competition?   _____

D. Noticing words: *(circle the words you hear/see)*

value	incentive	deposit	nature
invest	earn	sense	profit
amount	focus	loss	interest

E. Reading search:

1. How many words begin with 's'?   _____

2. Find a word that means 'got'.   _____

3. Find something that means 'not understanding'.   _____

4. Find a short word that collocates with 'believe'.   _____

5. Find two words that collocate with 'forget'.   _____

F. General questions:

1. What does Jin-Sook think would happen if everybody got the same amount of money ?

_____

2. What does Nazim think would happen if everybody got the same amount of money ?

_____

3. What does Jin-Sook think happens when we focus on money?

_____

G. Correct these statements:

1. Jin-Sook thinks money makes us lazy.

_____

2. Nazim thinks we need competition to encourage us to get up in the morning.

_____

3. Some people work hard because they like the elephants they are working with.

_____

H. Comprehension/personalization questions:

1. What does Jin-Sook think makes us greedy?

_____

2. What else do you think makes us greedy?

_____

3. What effect does Nazim think competition has?

_____

4. What other effect(s) do you think competition has?

_____

5. What does Jin-Sook think some people believe in?

_____

6. Give examples of what you believe in.

_____

3. Health

POINTS OF VIEW: Medical care should be free.

Before listening or reading

A. Warm-up questions:

1. How could medical care be made free for everybody?

_____

2. What would the bad points be if all doctors were employed by the government?

_____

3. What are the bad points when doctors have their own private hospitals?

_____

B. Anticipation gap-fill:

1. Health care is a basic human _____.

2. If they don't _____ good treatment, they lose patients.

3. Private doctors often _____ medicine for patients who are not really sick.

4. Young people have to _____ too much tax to support old people.

While listening or reading

Chen is the first and third speaker. Annan is the second and fourth speaker.

C. Listening/reading for gist:

1. Who thinks money should not decide who gets treatment?   _____

2. Who thinks market forces shouldn't be applied to health care?   _____

3. Who is against government health care?   _____

D. Noticing words: *(circle the words you hear/see)*

sore	prescribe	injury	treatment
insurance	dynamic	surgeries	toes
medicine	stiff	exercise	forces

E. Reading search:

1. How many words begin with 'p'?   _____

2. Find the opposite of 'lose money'.   _____

3. Find the opposite of 'in theory'.   _____

4. Find another way of saying 'medical care'.   _____

5. Find something that means 'government workers'.   _____

After listening or reading

F. General questions:

1. Why does Chen think medical care should be free for everybody?

_____

2. Why does Annan think market forces are effective?

_____

3. Who does Chen think private doctors often prescribe medicine for?

_____

G. Correct these statements:

1. Health care is a basic human left.

_____

2. Doctors sometimes refuse to give unnecessary birthday presents.

_____

3. Paying too much tax reduces our weight.

_____

H. Comprehension/personalization questions:

1. What does Chen think money should play no part in?

_____

2. What else do you think money should play no part in?

_____

3. What can be effective in keeping doctors on their toes?

_____

4. What's effective in keeping you on your toes?

_____

5. What is sometimes provided by governments?

_____

6. What else is sometimes provided by governments?

_____

4. Education

POINTS OF VIEW: Teachers should let students learn.

Before listening or reading

A. Warm-up questions:

1. Why do some teachers talk a lot in lessons?

_____

2. How can teachers motivate students more?

_____

3. Why do many students lose interest in school subjects?

_____

B. Anticipation gap-fill:

1. I'm fed _____ with listening to them.

2. The teacher would never get _____ the syllabus.

3. ... the only things most of us are interested in have nothing to _____ with school.

4. I'll teach in _____ the same way we have been taught.

While listening or reading

There are two students speaking. Answers should be 'The first student' or 'The second student'.

C. Listening/reading for gist:

1. Who thinks memorization is important?   _____

2. Who wants to be a teacher?   _____

3. Who thinks teachers need to motivate students more?   _____

D. Noticing words: *(circle the words you hear/see)*

graduate	curiosity	tests	syllabus
explaining	compulsory	exactly	herself
rule	freedom	imagination	bullying

E. Reading search:

1. How many words begin with 'c'?   _____

2. Find something that means 'discover things'.   _____

3. Find a word that collocates with 'get'.   _____

4. Find something that means 'ordering me'.   _____

5. Find two words that collocate with 'the same'.   _____

After listening or reading

F. General questions:

1. Why does the first student think teachers should stop explaining?

_____

2. Why does the second student think they have to memorize a lot of facts?

_____

3. Why does the first student think most students are not interested in school subjects?

_____

G. Correct these statements:

1. Teachers should stop telling students what to wear.

_____

2. Teachers need time to get through their lunch.

_____

3. The school system destroys students' sense of humor.

_____

H. Comprehension/personalization questions:

1. What will students have time to do in future?

_____

2. What do you hope you will have time to do in future?

_____

3. Name three things that have nothing to do with school.

_____

4. Name three things that have nothing to do with you.

_____

5. What worked for the second student?

_____

6. What way of learning English works best for you?

_____

5. Crime

POINTS OF VIEW: The death penalty is necessary.

Before listening or reading

A. Warm-up questions:

1. Why do some people support the death penalty?

_____

2. Why are some people against the death penalty?

_____

3. What do you think of the death penalty?

_____

B. Anticipation gap-fill:

1. If all murderers were executed, there'd be far _____ violent crime.

2. There's no evidence to _____ that the death penalty has any effect.

3. The only way to do this is by _____ murderers to death.

4. Shouldn't society be setting a better _____?

While listening or reading

Francesca is the first and third speaker. Abena is the second and fourth speaker.

C. Listening/reading for gist:

1. Who is in favor of the death penalty?   _____

2. Who thinks it's expensive to keep murderers alive?   _____

3. Who thinks the death penalty has a bad effect on society? _____

D. Noticing words: *(circle the words you hear/see)*

heat	prosecuted	motive	criminal
trial	innocent	court	consequences
convicted	consideration	suspected	noticeable

E. Reading search:

1. How many words begin with 's'?   _____

2. Find a word that means 'proof'.   _____

3. Find a word that collocates with 'consideration'. _____

4. Find a word that means 'on purpose'.   _____

5. Find the opposite of 'guilty'.   _____

After listening or reading

F. General questions:

1. What does Abena think most murderers don't consider?

_____

2. What does Francesca think may happen after murderers are released?

_____

3. What message does Abena think the death penalty sends to society?

_____

G. Correct these statements:

1. If somebody deliberately takes another person's dog, they have no right to live.

_____

2. Most killers become actors in the heat of the moment.

_____

3. Violence and killing are ways to deal with hunger.

_____

H. Comprehension/personalization questions:

1. What does Abena think there is no noticeable difference between?

_____

2. What do you feel there is no noticeable difference between?

_____

3. How does Francesca think we need to protect society?

_____

4. How else can we protect society?

_____

5. What do human beings sometimes have the right to do?

_____

6. What do you have the right to do?

_____

6. The Environment

POINTS OF VIEW: Rich countries have to take drastic action.

Before listening or reading

A. Warm-up questions:

1. How can rich countries prevent global warming?

_____

2. Where would the money come from?

_____

3. What will happen if not enough action is taken?

_____

B. Anticipation gap-fill:

1. … an international organization _____ up by the United Nations.

2. There are a lot of other things we have to _____ our money on.

3. The human race may not _____ much longer.

4. It's not as bad as all _____.

While listening or reading

Nazim is the first and third speaker. Francesca is the second and fourth speaker.

C. Listening/reading for gist:

1. Who is most concerned about the global environment?   _____

2. Who is most optimistic?   _____

3. Who thinks the United nations should play a key role?   _____

D. Noticing words: *(circle the words you hear/see)*

ozone	ecosystem	replant	survive
deforestation	emissions	organic	toxic
nuclear	greenhouse	exaggerating	pesticides

E. Reading search:

1. How many words begin with 'd'?   _____

2. Find something that means 'soon'.   _____

3. Find something that means 'meet each other'.   _____

4. Find the opposite of 'temporarily'.   _____

5. Find something that means 'it's better than that'.   _____

After listening or reading

F. General questions:

1. What does Nazim think the United Nations should do?

_____

2. What does Nazim think may happen to the human race?

_____

3. What is Francesca sure about?

_____

G. Correct these statements:

1. This organization would be responsible for causing problems.

_____

2. The polar bears will melt.

_____

3. More jokes will be made in the near future.

_____

H. Comprehension/personalization questions:

1. What would the new organization be responsible for?

_____

2. What are you responsible for?

_____

3. What will be permanently damaged?

_____

4. If you eat or drink too much or smoke, what may be permanently damaged?

_____

5. Who need to get together?

_____

6. Who would you like to get together with?

_____

7. Aliens

POINTS OF VIEW: There is intelligent life on other planets.

Before listening or reading

A. Warm-up questions:

1. State one argument that supports the existence of intelligent aliens.

_____

2. State one argument against the existence of intelligent aliens.

_____

3. State one reason why governments might keep the existence of aliens secret.

_____

B. Anticipation gap-fill:

1. The Earth is one small insignificant _____.

2. Astronomers have been looking for signs of intelligent life for _____.

3. There are so many reported _____ of UFOs.

4. If the government had _____ of UFOs, I'm sure they would tell us.

While listening or reading

Jin-Sook is the first and third speaker. Christina is the second and fourth speaker.

C. Listening/reading for gist:

1. Who thinks aliens have visited the Earth? _____

2. Who trusts her government more? _____

3. Who thinks there are intelligent aliens? _____

D. Noticing words: *(circle the words you hear/see)*

pace	evidence	hostile	galaxies
system	sightings	insignificant	fiction
dimension	beings	astronomers	advanced

E. Reading search:

1. How many words begin with 's'? _____

2. Find something that means 'flying saucers'. _____

3. Find the opposite of 'humble'. _____

4. Find two words that collocate with 'secret'. _____

5. Find two words that collocate with 'indications'. _____

After listening or reading

F. General questions:

1. What does Jin-Sook think it's arrogant to assume?

_____

2. What does Jin-Sook think governments keep secret?

_____

3. Why does Christina think her government wouldn't keep evidence secret?

_____

G. Correct these statements:

1. The earth is just one small arrogant planet.

_____

2. If there are intelligent aliens, some of them should have attacked us by now.

_____

3. There are so many reported sightings of dinosaurs.

_____

H. Comprehension/personalization questions:

1. If aliens are intelligent, what should they have done by now?

_____

2. If you are intelligent, what should you have done by now?

_____

3. What are there so may reported sightings of?

_____

4. List five other strange things that there have been many reported sightings of.

_____

5. What does Christina think wouldn't happen in a democratic society?

_____

6. What do you think wouldn't happen in a democratic society?

_____

8. History

POINTS OF VIEW: I admire Napoleon.

Before listening or reading

A. Warm-up questions:

1. Who was Napoleon?

_____

2. Name a female historical figure you respect.

_____

3. Why are most famous historical figures men?

_____

B. Anticipation gap-fill:

1. He could remember the names of _____ soldiers.

2. There wouldn't have been any wars in the first _____.

3. Female leaders have often been as aggressive as male leaders, if not _____ so.

4. It's not just _____ who says this.

While listening or reading

Annan is the first and third speaker. Christina is the second and fourth speaker.

C. Listening/reading for gist:

1. Who respects Napoleon? _____

2. Who thinks female leaders are not less aggressive? _____

3. Who respects a famous nurse? _____

D. Noticing words: *(circle the words you hear/see)*

tradition	period	religious	suffering
humane	legal	medieval	senseless
reform	freedom	ancient	sweeping

E. Reading search:

1. How many words begin with 'l'? _____

2. Find something that means 'equally'. _____

3. Find a word that means 'ruled'. _____

4. Find something that means 'a generalization'. _____

5. Find a word that means 'foundation'. _____

F. General questions:

1. Why does Annan think Napoleon was a great leader of men?

_____

2. What is Florence Nightingale famous for?

_____

3. Why does Christina think some female leaders are aggressive?

_____

G. Correct these statements:

1. Napoleon could remember the names of most of his children.

_____

2. Florence Nightingale started a great baseball tradition.

_____

3. Female leaders have often been just as romantic as male leaders.

_____

H. Comprehension/personalization questions:

1. What did Florence Nightingale take care of?

_____

2. Who or what do you have to take care of?

_____

3. What does Annan think is a sweeping statement?

_____

4. What would you like more time to do?

_____

5. What does Christina think would make the world more humane?

_____

6. What else do you think would make the world more humane?

_____

9. Women in Society

POINTS OF VIEW: Women don't have the same opportunities as men.

Before listening or reading

A. Warm-up questions:

1. Why do women tend to do more housework than men?

_____

2. Why are there fewer women than men in top management positions?

_____

3. Name one other way in which women are discriminated against.

_____

B. Anticipation gap-fill:

1. Most men still _____ us to do the housework.

2. Many women are often happy to _____ more attention to their families.

3. They are _____ to think that way from the moment they are born.

4. At least things are _____ than they used to be.

While listening or reading

Francesca is the first and third speaker. Manosh is the second and fourth speaker.

C. Listening/reading for gist:

1. Who has been married, Francesca or Manosh? _____

2. Who thinks many women are satisfied with their situations? _____

3. Who thinks women are conditioned by society? _____

D. Noticing words: *(circle the words you hear/see)*

discrimination	quota	appropriate	convenient
power	positions	managers	social
attention	harassment	action	supposed

E. Reading search:

1. How many words begin with 'h'? _____

2. Find a word that means 'senior'. _____

3. Find two words that collocate with 'way'. _____

4. Find a word that means 'understood'. _____

5. Find something that means 'focus on'. _____

After listening or reading

F. General questions:

1. What does Francesca think most men still expect?

_____

2. What does Manosh think many women are happy to do?

_____

3. What does Francesca think it's hard for women to do?

_____

G. Correct these statements:

1. Women are supposed to be more intelligent than men.

_____

2. Many women are often happy to pay attention to their pets.

_____

3. Women use hair conditioner from the moment they are born.

_____

H. Comprehension/personalization questions:

1. Who don't women have the same opportunities as?

_____

2. Who don't you have the same opportunities as?

_____

3. What does Francesca think is just an illusion?

_____

4. What else do you think is just an illusion?

_____

5. In what situation does Francesca think there's a lot of discrimination?

_____

6. Name another situation where you think there's a lot of discrimination.

_____

10. The Developing World

POINTS OF VIEW: Free trade makes everybody richer.

Before listening or reading

A. Warm-up questions:

1. Who do you think benefits most from free trade?

_____

2. What's your general impression of multinational companies?

_____

3. Why do companies from richer countries build factories in poorer countries?

_____

B. Anticipation gap-fill:

1. If every country in the world reduced import _____ …

2. Free trade _____ the rich richer and the poor poorer.

3. A strong world economy _____ everybody.

4. The aid does more _____ than good.

While listening or reading

Carlos is the first and third speaker. Abena is the second and fourth speaker.

C. Listening/reading for gist:

1. Who thinks free trade hurts developing countries? _____

2. Who thinks a strong world economy helps developing countries? _____

3. Who thinks multinationals exploit developing countries? _____

D. Noticing words: *(circle the words you hear/see)*

capital	charity	benefits	export
protect	hunger	corrupt	prevents
refugee	barriers	military	compete

E. Reading search:

1. How many words begin with 'g'? _____

2. Find a word that means 'stops'. _____

3. Find two words that collocate with 'provide'. _____

4. Find a word that collocates with 'export'. _____

5. Find a word that collocates with 'barriers'. _____

After listening or reading

F. General questions:

1. Why does Abena think free trade makes the rich richer?

_____

2. How can a strong world economy benefit developing countries?

_____

3. What do multinationals do when local salaries become higher?

_____

G. Correct these statements:

1. Free trade prevents multinationals from being able to protect their businesses.

_____

2. A strong world economy benefits politicians.

_____

3. As soon as local beaches become too popular, they move their factories to other countries.

_____

H. Comprehension/personalization questions:

1. What does Abena think widens the gap between rich and poor?

_____

2. What else do you think widens the gap between rich and poor?

_____

3. What does Carlos think provides well-paid jobs in developing countries?

_____

4. What else do you think provides well-paid jobs in developing countries?

_____

5. What does Abena think does more harm than good?

_____

6. What else do you think does more harm than good?

_____

11. Violence

POINTS OF VIEW: Violent sports should be banned.

Before listening or reading

A. Warm-up questions:

1. What influence do sports like boxing and wrestling have on children?

_____

2. Why are violent sports popular?

_____

3. How does the media influence the effect of violent sports?

_____

B. Anticipation gap-fill:

1. They send _____ a message that it's all right to fight.

2. There's going to be a certain _____ of violence in society whatever we do.

3. Violent _____ increases immediately after a televised boxing match.

4. That _____ more about the media than it does about boxing or wrestling.

While listening or reading

Tomoko is the first and third speaker. Chen is the second and fourth speaker.

C. Listening/reading for gist:

1. Who thinks the media sensationalizes violent sports? _____

2. Who thinks violent sports set a bad example? _____

3. Who thinks sport can be a substitute for war? _____

D. Noticing words: *(circle the words you hear/see)*

aggression	shocking	suicides	threaten
physical	irresponsible	message	outlet
prove	freedom	blood	televised

E. Reading search:

1. How many words begin with 'a'? _____

2. Find three words that collocate with 'violent'. _____

3. Find a pair of words that mean 'some'. _____

4. Find something that means 'transmit'. _____

5. Find something that means 'advertises a lot'. _____

After listening or reading

F. General questions:

1. Why does Tomoko think violent sports set a bad example?

_____

2. Why does Chen think many people wouldn't support Tomoko's argument?

_____

3. Why does Chen think it's unfair to ban physical sports?

_____

G. Correct these statements:

1. Boxing and wrestling send out a message that it's all right to murder people.

_____

2. There's going to be a certain amount of laziness in society whatever we do.

_____

3. If teachers didn't sensationalize exams, there wouldn't be any problem.

_____

H. Comprehension/personalization questions:

1. What does Tomoko think would happen if we banned violent sports?

_____

2. What else do you think would happen if we banned violent sports?

_____

3. What does Chen think sports provide an outlet for?

_____

4. Name an outlet you have when you feel violent or angry.

_____

5. What does Chen think the media should be blamed for?

_____

6. Name another negative effect the media has.

_____

12. Politics

POINTS OF VIEW: There should be no extremists.

Before listening or reading

A. Warm-up questions:

1. When do you think extremists are necessary, if ever?

_____

2. When do you think extremists might be dangerous?

_____

3. How can these dangers be reduced?

_____

B. Anticipation gap-fill:

1. There would be an election _____ four or five years.

2. What would happen if radical _____ was necessary?

3. ... would work well as long as there was _____ of speech.

4. We need ideology ... to give us all a _____ of purpose.

While listening or reading

Annan is the first and third speaker. Jin-Sook is the second and fourth speaker.

C. Listening/reading for gist:

1. Who thinks it's best to have some extremists? _____

2. Who thinks moderate political parties can be weak? _____

3. Who is against communist or military governments? _____

D. Noticing words: *(circle the words you hear/see)*

crisis	complacent	campaign	represented
genuine	ambitious	elect	majority
radical	candidate	contentious	anticipate

E. Reading search:

1. How many words begin with 'c'? _____

2. Find a word that means 'see in advance'. _____

3. Find a word that collocates with 'change'. _____

4. Find a word that means 'can be bribed'. _____

5. Find a word that collocates with 'issues'. _____

After listening or reading

F. General questions:

1. How often does Annan think there should be elections?

_____

2. What conditions does Annan feel are necessary for his idea to work well?

_____

3. What does Jin-Sook think moderate politicians are unlikely to anticipate?

_____

G. Correct these statements:

1. Extremists keep moderates on their stomachs.

_____

2. The system Annan's suggesting would lead to sensible arguments.

_____

3. Everything would be controlled by movie stars and aristocrats.

_____

H. Comprehension/personalization questions:

1. What do political parties do when they become comfortable?

_____

2. What do you do when you become comfortable?

_____

3. What do communist or military governments tend to be like?

_____

4. State another characteristic communist or military governments tend to have.

_____

5. What does Jin-Sook feel is not inspiring enough?

_____

6. What do you think is not inspiring enough?

_____

13. Economics

POINTS OF VIEW: Income taxes should be reduced.

Before listening or reading

A. Warm-up questions:

1. What are the advantages of reducing taxes?

_____

2. What are the disadvantages of reducing taxes?

_____

3. Why do indirect taxes generally hurt the poor more than direct taxes do?

_____

B. Anticipation gap-fill:

1. … production will increase, too, so unemployment will _____.

2. … demand for goods increases, so companies _____ up prices.

3. The immediate _____ of a reduction in income tax might be to …

4. … leads to more unemployment in the long _____.

While listening or reading

Abena is the first and third speaker. Christina is the second and fourth speaker.

C. Listening/reading for gist:

1. Who is worried about inflation?   _____

2. Who's in favor of stimulating production and consumption?   _____

3. Who is most concerned about how the poor are affected?   _____

D. Noticing words: *(circle the words you hear/see)*

boost	deficit	weaken	factors
supply	progressive	demand	innovation
reduced	cautious	profitable	slightly

E. Reading search:

1. How many words begin with 'i'?   _____

2. Find a word that means 'lead to'.   _____

3. Find a word that means 'decrease'.   _____

4. Find a word that means 'a little'.   _____

5. Find an example of a direct tax.   _____

After listening or reading

F. General questions:

1. Why might an increase in consumption help the economy?

_____

2. Why might an increase in consumption hurt the economy?

_____

3. Why does income tax that is progressive benefit the poor?

_____

G. Correct these statements:

1. Both these actors lead to an increase in inflation.

_____

2. If GNP is higher, the government will get more income from bribes.

_____

3. Inflation hurts managers more than those with part-time jobs.

_____

H. Comprehension/personalization questions:

1. What happens to pay when unemployment falls?

_____

2. What else happens when unemployment falls?

_____

3. What does Abena think the long-term effect of an income tax reduction would be?

_____

4. What do you think the long-term effect of a reduction in your weight would be?

_____

5. What does Christina think should be increased?

_____

6. What else do you think should be increased?

_____

14. Happiness

POINTS OF VIEW: I wish I could have a good time.

Before listening or reading

A. Warm-up questions:

1. How would you feel if you lived on a beautiful island for the rest of your life?

_____

2. What gives you a sense of purpose in life?

_____

3. What could you do to help improve society?

_____

B. Anticipation gap-fill:

1. I can think of nothing _____ than to be surrounded by beautiful things.

2. The kind of satisfaction you're talking about doesn't _____ long.

3. You don't need to sit in an office in order to _____ a purpose in life.

4. They're all concerned with the immediate _____ around us.

While listening or reading

Tomoko is the first and third speaker. Nazim is the second and fourth speaker.

C. Listening/reading for gist:

1. Who thinks there are many things to do on an island?   _____

2. Who wants to contribute the most to society?   _____

3. Who is most interested in having a good time?   _____

D. Noticing words: *(circle the words you hear/see)*

wide	fulfilling	goal	while
direction	complain	whole	satisfied
surrounded	senses	miss	achievement

E. Reading search:

1. How many words begin with 'i'?   _____

2. Find something that means 'bring up'.   _____

3. Find a word that means 'encircled'.   _____

4. Find something that means 'a period of time'.   _____

5. Find three words that collocate with 'ways'.   _____

After listening or reading

F. General questions:

1. What isn't enough for Nazim?

_____

2. What don't we need to do in order to find a purpose in life?

_____

3. What does Nazim think is wrong with the ways of living Tomoko suggests?

_____

G. Correct these statements:

1. Tomoko wishes she could live forever on a romantic Arctic island.

_____

2. Nazim feels he'd be wasting his money on a romantic island.

_____

3. Tomoko thinks Nazim could raise some happy animals on the island.

_____

H. Comprehension/personalization questions:

1. What does Nazim think would be great for a while?

_____

2. What do you think would be great for a while?

_____

3. State two of Tomoko's ideas for ways of finding happiness on an island.

_____

4. State two other ways to find happiness on an island that Tomoko didn't mention.

_____

5. What wider goal does Nazim have?

_____

6. State a wider goal that you have.

_____

15. Globalization

POINTS OF VIEW: Learning about the world makes us international.

Before listening or reading

A. Warm-up questions:

1. What do we need to do to become more international?

_____

2. In which ways may school help us become more international?

_____

3. In which ways may school make us less international?

_____

B. Anticipation gap-fill:

1. I've had itchy _____ ever since.

2. … and yet seem to be able to accept different _____ of thinking.

3. I guess a lot of people don't take _____ of the opportunities they have.

4. We could then _____ our potential as full members of …

While listening or reading

Chen is the first and third speaker. Manosh is the second and fourth speaker.

C. Listening/reading for gist:

1. Who thinks school may do more harm than good?   _____

2. Who thinks travel broadens the mind?   _____

3. Who emphasizes the importance of mental flexibility?   _____

D. Noticing words: *(circle the words you hear/see)*

advantage	outlook	questioning	across
exposure	suppressed	straightforward	global
cosmopolitan	nationalistic	prejudice	deeper

E. Reading search:

1. How many words begin with 's'?   _____

2. Find something that means 'give the impression'.   _____

3. Find a word that means 'basics'.   _____

4. Find something that means 'originally'.   _____

5. Find a word that means 'clear cut'.   _____

After listening or reading

F. General questions:

1. How do some people who have traveled a lot come across to Manosh?

_____

2. What does Chen think is the key to making our society more international?

_____

3. What does Manosh think the focus on knowledge does to our curiosity?

_____

G. Correct these statements:

1. If he hadn't traveled, Chen would probably still have an itchy view of the world.

_____

2. Some people who have traveled a lot come across as being very jet-lagged.

_____

3. We are born with flexible and curious legs.

_____

H. Comprehension/personalization questions:

1. What is Chen interested in doing for himself?

_____

2. What are you interested in doing for yourself?

_____

3. Who does Manosh often run into?

_____

4. Who do you often run into?

_____

5. What does Manosh think we have the potential to be?

_____

6. What else do you think we have the potential to be?

_____

1. Attitudes

A. Fill in the blanks with a possible word:

1. I have these deep emotional _____.

2. I'm about as _____ as they come. I'm negative about the future.

3. I think I'm _____. I feel everybody is against me.

4. The _____ thing is it will probably become true.

5. You can find a _____ to make it work if you want to.

6. You should both go _____ your relationship with a positive attitude.

7. We'll have to accept that our ways of _____ are very different.

8. My prejudice against female managers is very deep-_____.

9. I don't know whether I'm coming or _____.

10. I don't mind what happens. I couldn't care _____.

B. Complete these sentences with your own ideas:

1. I'm optimistic about _____

2. I need to take a close look at _____

3. I don't like the way _____

4. I feel disappointed when _____

5. I try to look on the bright side when _____

C. Quiz:

1. Name somewhere where there's a lot of prejudice.   _____

2. Name a politician who is indecisive.   _____

3. Name a friend who is easygoing.   _____

4. Name a famous person who has a patronizing attitude.   _____

5. Name a scientist that was good at lateral thinking.   _____

D. Jumbled up sentences:

1. without she people I've hesitation always believes imagined.
I've _____

2. to person seems as me everybody broad-minded see a.
Everybody _____

3. feel the help way can't we we.
We _____

4. a attitude my way I I could find to wish change.
I _____

5. nerves new on gets boss my my.
My _____

E. Sentences from words: *(write sentences that include these words)*

1. tolerant

_____

2. narrow-minded

_____

3. argument

_____

4. responsible

_____

5. overcome

_____

F. Writing dialogues: *(write at least an eight-line dialogue for each situation)*

1. Advise a friend who is lonely.

_____
_____
_____
_____
_____
_____
_____

2. Interview a pessimistic superstar.

_____
_____
_____
_____
_____
_____
_____
_____

1. Attitudes

3. Interview a different superstar who is optimistic.

_____
_____
_____
_____
_____
_____
_____
_____

Unit Assessment

G. Word search:

P	A	T	R	O	N	I	Z	I	N	G	D
R	T	W	U	D	E	C	I	S	I	V	E
E	T	P	A	R	A	N	O	I	D	Y	X
J	E	A	T	T	I	T	U	D	E	K	P
U	N	R	J	M	L	Q	P	N	F	L	E
D	T	G	H	F	S	I	M	I	L	A	R
I	I	U	T	O	L	E	R	A	N	T	I
C	O	M	M	U	N	I	C	A	T	E	E
E	N	E	S	V	P	W	N	G	T	R	N
H	X	N	E	G	A	T	I	V	E	A	C
O	P	T	I	M	I	S	T	I	C	L	E
E	A	S	Y	G	O	I	N	G	P	N	F

There are 15 words from Unit 1 hidden in this puzzle. Can you find them? They are written either across, CAT, or down, C. The shortest word has seven letters.
A
T

_____   _____
_____   _____
_____   _____
_____   _____
_____   _____
_____   _____

H. Hidden message:

1	2	3	4		5 T	6 o	7 m	6 o	8 k	6 o	,

2. Money

A. Fill in the blanks with a possible word:

1. If I leave it in the bank, it won't earn much _____.

2. You run the _____ of losing a lot of money.

3. She thinks we should all get _____ the same amount of money.

4. Competition is part of human _____.

5. I believe in the social _____ of what I'm doing.

6. The _____ of our lives will suffer.

7. You are missing the _____.

8. If we have a concert, we'll be able to _____ a lot of money for charity.

9. Buying them dinner is a small _____ to pay for getting the contract.

10. You should save your winnings for a _____ day.

B. Complete these sentences with your own ideas:

1. If I invest in the stock market _____

2. I tend to focus on _____

3. I waste money when _____

4. I'd like to earn a living by _____

5. When I'm in debt I _____

C. Quiz:

1. Name a company that makes a large profit.   _____

2. Name a company that makes a big loss.   _____

3. Name a famous person who seems very greedy.   _____

4. Name a product that has a low profit margin.   _____

5. Name a country that is heavily in debt.   _____

D. Jumbled up sentences:

1. in point leaving bank there's the it in no.

There's _____

2. work all same people amount hard if wouldn't the many got we.

If _____

3. of work of some responsibility hard sense out a people.

Some _____

4. be gross net less profit a profit than lot the the will.

The _____

5. are think tough people things most finding I.

I _____

2. Money

E. Sentences from words: *(write sentences that include these words)*

1. incentive

_____

2. value

_____

3. deposit

_____

4. frankly

_____

5. range

_____

F. Writing dialogues: *(write at least an eight-line dialogue for each situation)*

1. Advise a friend who wants to start a business.

_____

_____

_____

_____

_____

_____

_____

_____

2. Try to sell your computer to a second-hand shop.

_____

_____

_____

_____

_____

_____

_____

_____

Unit Assessment

3. Interview a very successful businessman/woman.

_____

_____

_____

_____

_____

_____

_____

_____

G. Word search:

C	O	N	P	S	W	A	S	T	E	O	B
O	X	A	J	W	O	N	J	I	B	S	U
M	L	M	K	T	R	P	D	Z	U	J	S
P	R	O	F	I	T	X	N	W	D	B	I
E	U	U	O	P	H	M	A	R	G	I	N
T	L	N	C	A	P	I	T	A	L	I	E
I	F	T	U	I	L	W	C	X	G	N	S
T	Q	P	S	K	D	Q	H	N	R	V	S
I	N	C	E	N	T	I	V	E	E	E	I
V	K	B	N	I	N	T	E	R	E	S	T
E	D	E	P	O	S	I	T	M	D	T	J
R	B	A	S	I	C	A	L	L	Y	H	K

There are 15 words from Unit 2 hidden in this puzzle. Can you find them? They are written either across, CAT, or down, C. The shortest word has five letters.
A
T

_____   _____

_____   _____

_____   _____

_____   _____

_____   _____

_____   _____

_____

H. Hidden message:

1	2	3	4		5 M	3 a	6 n	7 o	8 s	9 h	,															
10	2		3	4	2		5	3	11	12	6	13		3		14 p	4 r	7 o	15 f	12 i	16 t		3	16		16 9 2
5	7	5	2	6	16	,		17	18	16		6	7	16		2	6	7	18	13	9		16	7		4 12 8 11
12	6	19	2	8	16	12	6	13		12	6		16	9	2		8	16	7	20	11		5	3	4 11 2 16 .	12 16
10	7	18	21	1		22	18	8	16		17	2		3		10	3	8	16	2		7	15		5 7 6 2 23 .	12 16
1	7	2	8	6	,	16		13	4	7	10		7	6		16	4	2	8	,		23	7	18	11 6 7 10 !	12
16	9	12	6	11		3		8	9	7	18	21	1		22	18	8	16		8	3	19	2		12 16 15 7 4	3
4	3	12	6	23	.		1	3	23	.		15	4	3	6	20	2	8	20	3						

3. Health

A. Fill in the blanks with a possible word:

1. My body _____ all over.

2. Jogging can do more _____ than good.

3. You'll feel better in no _____.

4. I could easily get a _____ all over my arms.

5. Health care is a basic human _____.

6. It wouldn't work in _____.

7. When market forces are _____ to health care, it leads to waste.

8. The government can't afford to _____ free health care.

9. He _____ his health, so it's not surprising he's sick.

10. It was just a _____ of the tongue.

B. Complete these sentences with your own ideas:

1. I need to take out insurance for _____

2. I sometimes get a rash _____

3. Money should play no part in _____

4. The government can't afford to _____

5. I take care of my health by _____

C. Quiz:

1. Name a medicine that cures headaches.   _____

2. Name a harmful side effect of smoking.   _____

3. Name a treatment for a stiff shoulder.   _____

4. Name a country where most health care is free.   _____

5. Name a country that has very high tax.   _____

D. Jumbled up sentences:

1. have most side even ointments common effects and serious the can creams.
   Even _____

2. on forces effective keeping toes in their market doctors be can.
   Market _____

3. patient refuses treatment a doctors the change give if unnecessary to will doctor.
   If _____

4. economy support the taxes dynamic people make less old to.
   Taxes _____

5. out just other ear one arguments the your and in go.
   Your _____

E. Sentences from words: *(write sentences that include these words)*

1. prescribe

_____

2. swollen

_____

3. injury

_____

4. emergency

_____

5. unexpected

_____

F. Writing dialogues: *(write at least an eight-line dialogue for each situation)*

1. You always feel tired, and are asking a doctor for help.

_____

_____

_____

_____

_____

_____

_____

_____

2. Question the advice of a doctor who is suggesting you take more exercise.

_____

_____

_____

_____

_____

_____

_____

_____

3. Health

3. Interview a very rich doctor.

_____

_____

_____

_____

_____

_____

_____

Unit Assessment

G. Word search:

U	B	I	N	S	U	R	A	N	C	E	S
N	K	T	J	U	Y	W	C	M	W	K	W
N	S	R	P	R	O	V	I	D	E	N	O
E	M	E	R	G	E	N	C	Y	P	C	L
C	J	A	N	E	G	L	E	C	T	D	L
E	F	T	P	R	E	S	C	R	I	B	E
S	T	M	H	I	N	J	U	R	Y	H	N
S	M	E	M	E	D	I	C	I	N	E	T
A	X	N	V	S	P	A	T	I	E	N	T
R	L	T	L	E	X	E	R	C	I	S	E
Y	A	L	L	E	R	G	I	E	S	P	Z
A	C	C	O	R	D	I	N	G	Y	M	J

There are 15 words from Unit 3 hidden in this puzzle. Can you find them? They are written either across, CAT, or down, C. The shortest word has six letters.

A
T

_____   _____

_____   _____

_____   _____

_____   _____

_____   _____

_____   _____

H. Hidden message:

4. Education

A. Fill in the blanks with a possible word:

1. My school was _____. There were no boys.

2. Most of us were _____ to study at home by ourselves.

3. There was nothing to _____ us to study for ourselves.

4. She wants to find things out for _____.

5. I wish they would let me think things _____.

6. I'd learn a lot more that _____.

7. It's _____ because of the way we were taught.

8. We only employ _____ teachers with a professional attitude.

9. The lesson was way over my _____.

10. There was nobody to teach us, so we had to learn from _____.

B. Complete these sentences with your own ideas:

1. I sometimes memorize _____

2. Freedom of choice _____

3. I'll never get a chance to know much about _____

4. If I have time to find things out for myself _____

5. An experienced teacher _____

C. Quiz:

1. Name a compulsory school subject in your country. _____

2. Name a famous co-educational school. _____

3. Name something that has nothing to do with school. _____

4. Name a conscientious teacher. _____

5. Name an actor who's in a class of his own. _____

D. Jumbled up sentences:

1. learned wonder much we often very if I.
   I _____

2. study themselves were at of motivated most by them home to.
   Most _____

3. hierarchy strictness bullying led lot the to and of a.
   The _____

4. do they explaining to stop all is have.
   All _____

5. our system curiosity school creativity destroys and the.
   The _____

4. Education

E. Sentences from words: *(write sentences that include these words)*

1. syllabus

_____

2. bullying

_____

3. teacher-centered

_____

4. retake

_____

5. qualified

_____

F. Writing dialogues: *(write at least an eight-line dialogue for each situation)*

1. Explain to your teacher why you were absent from class.

_____

_____

_____

_____

_____

_____

_____

_____

2. Give advice to a student about his/her future.

_____

_____

_____

_____

_____

_____

_____

_____

3. Discuss the qualities of a good teacher.

_____

_____

_____

_____

_____

_____

_____

_____

G. Word search:

N	G	C	U	R	R	I	C	U	L	U	M
J	C	O	B	S	K	V	R	B	P	C	Q
M	E	M	O	R	I	Z	E	U	X	U	U
O	N	P	D	E	K	Z	A	L	S	R	A
T	T	U	I	X	L	G	T	L	Y	I	L
I	E	L	S	A	F	R	I	Y	L	O	I
V	R	S	C	C	D	A	V	I	L	S	F
A	E	O	O	T	W	D	I	N	A	I	I
T	D	R	V	L	Y	U	T	G	B	T	E
I	M	Y	E	Y	J	A	Y	Q	U	Y	D
O	S	T	R	I	C	T	N	E	S	S	L
N	W	S	U	B	J	E	C	T	F	D	M

There are 15 words from Unit 4 hidden in this puzzle. Can you find them? They are written either across, CAT, or down, C. The shortest word has seven letters.
$$\begin{matrix} A \\ T \end{matrix}$$

_____   _____

_____   _____

_____   _____

_____   _____

_____   _____

_____   _____

_____   _____

_____

H. Hidden message:

1	2	3	4		3 A	5 b	2 e	6 n	3 a	,															
7		8	9	6	1	2	4		7	10		9	11	4		12	2	3	13	14	2	4	,	15	
16	11	3	17	7	10	7	2	1	.		14	7	15		17	2	15	15	9	6	15		3	4	2
9	11	4		14	2	3	1	15	,		3	6	1			1	9	6	,	12		12	14	7	6
10	9	17	17	9	8	7	6	20		3		15	18	17	17	3	5	11	15		3	6	1		12
1	3	18		14	2		2	21	2	6		3	15	19	2	1		10	9	4		3	17	17	
12	2	17	2	22	14	9	6	2		6	11	23	5	2	4	15	.		12	14	7	15		7	15
15	7	6	20	17	2	_	15	2	24		20 g	7 i	4 r	17 l	15 s	,		15	13	14	9	9	17	!	25

5. Crime

Unit Assessment

A. Fill in the blanks with a possible word:

1. There was no _____ to prove she was guilty.

2. I couldn't prove I wasn't there. I had no _____ .

3. I had to appear in court, but fortunately I was found _____ .

4. He was _____ to ten years in prison.

5. If murderers were executed, there'd be far less _____ crime.

6. A far more important _____ is that the death penalty sets a bad example.

7. It says that human beings have the _____ to take other people's lives.

8. The crime _____ continues to increase.

9. The police have _____ many suspects.

10. You deserve it. It _____ you right.

B. Complete these sentences with your own ideas:

1. I once suspected _____

2. There is evidence to show that _____

3. We have the right to _____

4. The police recently arrested _____

5. I sometimes jump to conclusions when _____

C. Quiz:

1. Name a politician who committed a crime.   _____

2. Name a famous criminal.   _____

3. Name a country that does not have the death penalty.   _____

4. Name somebody who was sentenced to death.   _____

5. Name a famous long court case.   _____

D. Jumbled up sentences:

1. a witness search through her computer a identified.
   A _____

2. a was criminal as years branded few a he for.
   He _____

3. to deliberately no somebody they live if right takes have person's life another.
   If _____

4. another tells life of take penalty that every human member OK the to society it's death being's.
   The _____

5. companies the court to have of agreed out two settle.
   The _____

E. Sentences from words: *(write sentences that include these words)*

1. convicted

_____

2. motive

_____

3. prosecuted

_____

4. branded

_____

5. consequences

_____

F. Writing dialogues: *(write at least an eight-line dialogue for each situation)*

1. Explain to a policeman/woman why you are carrying a gun.

_____

_____

_____

_____

_____

_____

_____

_____

2. Argue that a robber shouldn't go to prison.

_____

_____

_____

_____

_____

_____

_____

_____

5. Crime

3. Discuss what should happen to somebody who murdered your teacher.

_____
_____
_____
_____
_____
_____
_____
_____

Unit Assessment

G. Word search:

C	M	U	R	D	E	R	E	R	J	B	Z
O	S	X	K	E	V	I	D	E	N	C	E
N	S	N	V	L	J	W	P	I	C	B	P
S	U	S	P	I	C	I	O	N	R	R	R
E	S	E	R	B	O	T	G	N	I	A	O
Q	P	N	O	E	N	N	H	O	M	N	S
U	I	T	T	R	V	E	P	C	I	D	E
E	C	E	E	A	I	S	W	E	N	E	C
N	I	N	C	T	C	S	L	N	A	D	U
C	O	C	T	E	T	S	V	T	L	K	T
E	N	E	M	L	E	M	O	T	I	V	E
S	F	D	V	Y	D	A	L	I	B	I	D

There are 15 words from Unit 5 hidden in this puzzle. Can you find them? They are written either across, CAT, or down, C. The shortest word has five letters.
A
T

_____   _____
_____   _____
_____   _____
_____   _____
_____   _____
_____   _____
_____

H. Hidden message:

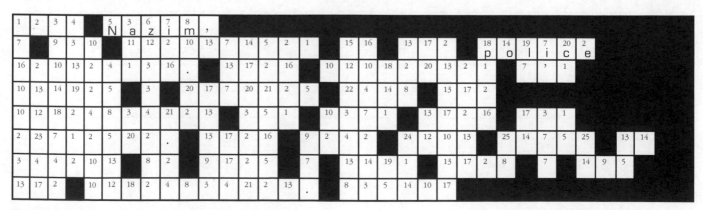

6. The Environment

A. Fill in the blanks with a possible word:

1. Global _____ is caused by the greenhouse effect.

2. Many problems are the _____ effects of industrialization.

3. We have to replant the rain _____.

4. The United Nations should set _____ an international organization.

5. The _____ layer is getting thinner.

6. It's not as bad as _____ that.

7. We all need to get _____ and agree on new policies.

8. When we moved to the city we had to _____ to the new environment.

9. There was a _____ view of the mountains from our window.

10. You shouldn't make a mountain out of a _____.

B. Complete these sentences with your own ideas:

1. Global warming can be reduced if _____

2. I'd like to radically change _____

3. We need to deal with problems like _____

4. The human race will not survive long if _____

5. I wasn't my fault that _____

C. Quiz:

1. Name an area where there's a lot of acid rain.   _____

2. Name a country that's exploited by others.   _____

3. Name the Secretary General of the UN.   _____

4. Name an animal that adapts to new environments well.   _____

5. Name a place with a breathtaking view.   _____

D. Jumbled up sentences:

1. make cut dioxide if much it carbon even won't down difference on we.
Even _____

2. destroyed may ecosystem the permanently we earth's have.
We _____

3. change at life chance radically to way have our all of any to we stand.
To _____

4. too of people don't radiation we many ultra-violet something much cancer will by caused die if do.
If _____

5. of is the get things iceberg – this the are worse tip going just to.
This _____

6. The Environment

Unit Assessment

E. Sentences from words: *(write sentences that include these words)*

1. emissions

_____

2. toxic

_____

3. ingredients

_____

4. habitat

_____

5. block

_____

F. Writing dialogues: *(write at least an eight-line dialogue for each situation)*

1. Try to persuade a friend to eat only organically grown food.

_____

_____

_____

_____

_____

_____

_____

_____

2. Try to persuade the President/Prime Minister to ban cars.

_____

_____

_____

_____

_____

_____

_____

_____

3. Discuss the consequences of global warming with a friend.

_____

_____

_____

_____

_____

_____

_____

G. Word search:

E	C	O	S	Y	S	T	E	M	C	P	B
X	D	R	A	S	T	I	C	J	O	E	R
A	W	G	M	I	H	H	O	G	N	R	E
G	A	A	P	C	A	F	Z	C	S	M	A
G	R	N	E	E	B	W	O	B	U	A	T
E	M	I	S	B	I	Q	N	N	M	N	H
R	I	C	T	E	T	T	E	B	E	E	T
A	N	G	I	R	A	O	M	K	R	N	A
T	G	J	C	G	T	X	K	P	I	T	K
I	E	M	I	S	S	I	O	N	S	L	I
N	N	K	D	L	V	C	J	F	M	Y	N
G	R	E	E	N	H	O	U	S	E	K	G

There are 15 words from Unit 6 hidden in this puzzle. Can you find them? They are written either across, CAT, or down, C. The shortest word has five letters.
A
T

_____   _____

_____   _____

_____   _____

_____   _____

_____   _____

_____   _____

_____   _____

_____

H. Hidden message:

(puzzle grid with numbered cells; filled letters read "Carlos," at top, and "view" in a lower row)

7. Aliens

Unit Assessment

A. Fill in the blanks with a possible word:

1. UFOs probably travel faster than the speed of _____.

2. Not many planets are able to _____ human life.

3. New technology may _____ us to travel to another dimension.

4. It's arrogant to _____ we are the only intelligent beings.

5. _____ are always searching for new planets and intelligent life.

6. There are many reported _____ of UFOs.

7. Governments keep their knowledge _____.

8. Earth and Mars are planets in the _____ system.

9. Whether or not there was life on Mars will probably _____ a mystery.

10. Your _____ is as good as mine.

B. Complete these sentences with your own ideas:

1. The biggest problem I have to overcome is _____

2. By now, I should be able to _____

3. I don't have enough space to _____

4. I think solar energy _____

5. It's a complete mystery to me why/that _____

C. Quiz:

1. Name a famous science fiction writer. _____

2. Name the furthest planet in the solar system. _____

3. Name a mystery that was solved. _____

4. Name some recently developed technology. _____

5. Name a famous astronomer. _____

D. Jumbled up sentences:

1. identify will human that can astronomers life to support planets have.
   Astronomers _____

2. many must read it novels like too sound detective I.
   I _____

3. really probably ready government know we're on to what's the going not thinks.
   The _____

4. very was couldn't that's myself say express what well but trying I to I.
   I _____

5. must the happens of continue exploration whatever space.
   The _____

E. Sentences from words: *(write sentences that include these words)*

1. galaxy

_____

2. sightings

_____

3. insignificant

_____

4. universe

_____

5. powered

_____

F. Writing dialogues: *(write at least an eight-line dialogue for each situation)*

1. Interview a homesick alien.

_____
_____
_____
_____
_____
_____
_____
_____

2. You are an alien asking questions about the Earth.

_____
_____
_____
_____
_____
_____
_____
_____

7. Aliens

3. Discuss with a friend whether aliens have visited the Earth.

_____

_____

_____

_____

_____

_____

_____

G. Word search:

A	S	S	U	M	E	G	H	T	W	O	G
S	N	H	L	K	S	O	L	A	R	V	D
T	E	C	H	N	O	L	O	G	Y	E	I
R	G	F	C	O	S	A	U	C	E	R	M
O	D	E	B	W	H	L	W	Q	N	C	E
N	E	X	P	L	O	R	A	T	I	O	N
O	F	D	R	E	O	U	T	E	R	M	S
M	A	Z	N	D	F	R	P	M	D	E	I
E	L	S	I	G	H	T	I	N	G	S	O
R	I	W	R	E	P	O	R	T	E	D	N
B	E	M	W	J	M	Y	S	T	E	R	Y
U	N	I	V	E	R	S	E	R	P	K	V

There are 15 words from Unit 7 hidden in this puzzle. Can you find them? They are written either across, CAT, or down, C. The shortest word has five letters.
A
T

_____   _____

_____   _____

_____   _____

_____   _____

_____   _____

_____   _____

_____   _____

_____

H. Hidden message:

1	2	3	4		5	6	2	7		,																		
8	,	9	2		10	2	2	7		8	7		3		11	12	13	8	7	14		15	3	16	5	2	4	!
															f	l	y	i	n	g								
3	12	8	2	7	15		3	10	1	16	5	17	2	1		18	2		3	7	1		17	19	19	20		18	2		3	17
17	6	2		15	21	2	2	1		19	11		12	8	14	6	17		8	7	17	19		19	16	17	2	4
15	21	3	5	2			22	2		2	9	2	7		9	8	15	8	17	2	1		3	7	19	17	6	2	4
1	8	18	2	7	15	8	19	7		.		17	6	2	13		10	4	19	16	14	6	17		18	2		10	3	5	20
22	6	2	7		17	6	2	13		11	19	16	7	1		8		22	3	15	7	,	17		17	6	2
3	18	2	4	8	5	3	7		21	4	2	15	8	1	2	7	17		.		3	7	7	3	7

8. History

A. Fill in the blanks with a possible word:

1. The _____ system was common in the medieval period.

2. Members of the _____ lived healthier lives than ordinary people.

3. The _____ revolution led to a lot of suffering in factories.

4. _____ were exploited by the richer countries.

5. Napoleon introduced a _____ system that is the basis of European law.

6. It's a very _____ statement to say wars are caused by individuals.

7. Great leaders can change the _____ of history.

8. He's going through a very _____ period in our lives.

9. Nobody believed that war would really _____ out.

10. It's just a _____ of time before our boss finds out.

B. Complete these sentences with your own ideas:

1. I wish I could have lived _____

2. During the medieval period _____

3. During the industrial revolution _____

4. Wars are usually caused by _____

5. It's not only me who says that _____

C. Quiz:

1. Name a great reformer.   _____

2. Name a leader who changed the course of history.   _____

3. Name a country that is run by a woman now.   _____

4. Name an ancient female leader.   _____

5. Name a famous civil war.   _____

D. Jumbled up sentences:

1. challenged have the it to being would feudal wonderful see system been.
   It _____

2. other aristocrats wars constantly countries most up were with caught in.
   Most _____

3. and responsible killing and so suffering generals much for are admirals.
   Generals _____

4. were the if place women wouldn't run wars countries any by first be in there.
   There _____

5. believed effective threat it war the an often deterrent that is of is.
   It _____

8. History

E. Sentences from words: *(write sentences that include these words)*

1. colony

_____

2. revolution

_____

3. reform

_____

4. period

_____

5. ordinary

_____

F. Writing dialogues: *(write at least an eight-line dialogue for each situation)*

1. Argue with a friend about who was the greatest leader in your country.

_____

_____

_____

_____

_____

_____

_____

2. Argue with a friend about whether to fight in a war.

_____

_____

_____

_____

_____

_____

_____

3. Discuss with a friend what it was like to live five hundred years ago.

_____

_____

_____

_____

_____

_____

_____

G. Word search:

R	E	F	O	R	M	A	T	I	O	N	I
E	O	R	D	I	N	A	R	Y	X	Y	N
N	K	R	E	V	O	L	U	T	I	O	N
A	R	I	S	T	O	C	R	A	C	Y	O
I	N	M	W	N	P	E	R	I	O	D	V
S	W	E	E	P	I	N	G	B	P	F	A
S	H	D	C	O	L	O	N	I	E	S	T
A	G	I	H	F	E	U	D	A	L	W	I
N	S	E	N	S	E	L	E	S	S	K	O
C	I	V	I	L	I	Z	A	T	I	O	N
E	F	A	N	C	I	E	N	T	L	G	B
D	J	L	T	R	A	D	I	T	I	O	N

There are 15 words from Unit 8 hidden in this puzzle. Can you find them? They are written either across, CAT, or down, C.
A
T
The shortest word has six letters.

_____   _____

_____   _____

_____   _____

_____   _____

_____   _____

_____   _____

_____

H. Hidden message:

1	2	3	4		5	6	4	7	8	9	7	10	3		,													
7	11		7		12	3	8		13	7	14	7	10	15		7	10		9	6	2		16	2	1	7	2	14	3	13
17	2	4	7	18	1		,		7	,	1		19	2		3		20	10	7	15	6	9		7	10		8	6	7	10	7	10	15
3	4	16	18	4		.		7	,	1		19	2		14	2	4	21		19	4	3	14	2		3	10	1		11	7	15	6	9
9	18		4	2	11	18	4	16		9	6	2		11	2	22	1	3	13		8	21	8	9	2	16		8	18		3	13	13
17	2	18	17	13	2		5	18	22	13	1		19	2		2	23	22	3	13		2	14	2	4	21	19	18	1	21
12	18	22	13	1		8	3	21		7		12	3	8		3		15	18	18	1		20	10	7	15	6	9		.		15	18	18	1
10	7	15	6	9	!		5	3	4	13	18	8																	

(In the hidden message grid, the partially filled word reads: **k n i g h t**)

9. Women in Society

A. Fill in the blanks with a possible word:

1. Our society is very male _____.

2. Men and women should accept that we are _____ different.

3. We need _____ action to achieve more equality.

4. When we were married, we went out once a year at _____.

5. Many women are happy to _____ their male bosses.

6. That way of thinking is just an illusion that's _____ for men.

7. Women are _____ to think like that from the moment they are born.

8. There's a _____ of opportunity now, but the chance won't last long.

9. A woman's _____ is in the home.

10. _____ are a man's best friend.

B. Complete these sentences with your own ideas:

1. I've been conditioned to _____

2. I should accept that _____

3. I'm happy to _____

4. I've wasted opportunities to _____

5. I think sexual harassment _____

C. Quiz:

1. Name a custom that discriminates against women.   _____

2. Name a woman who has got to the top.   _____

3. Name a country where men and women are reasonably equal.   _____

4. Name a self-made man/woman.   _____

5. Name a male chauvinist.   _____

D. Jumbled up sentences:

1. all about fact opportunity power people men equal the talk have in but.
People _____

2. female action of ensure managers we quota affirmative there's to a need.
We _____

3. attention to families who jobs many more have women responsible their pay don't.
Many _____

4. sexual the lot there's harassment discrimination way a along and of.
There's _____

5. my play woman right right if I'll my boss' I hand become cards.
If _____

E. Sentences from words: *(write sentences that include these words)*

1. appropriate

_____

2. quota

_____

3. illusion

_____

4. acceptable

_____

5. granted

_____

F. Writing dialogues: *(write at least an eight-line dialogue for each situation)*

1. Talk with a woman you are considering employing in a job usually done by men.

_____

_____

_____

_____

_____

_____

_____

_____

2. Discuss with a friend whether there are differences between men and women.

_____

_____

_____

_____

_____

_____

_____

_____

3. Boast to a friend about the qualities of your boyfriend/girlfriend.

_____

_____

_____

_____

_____

_____

_____

G. Word search:

```
A F F I R M A T I V E G
P C O N D I T I O N E D
P H B N I L L U S I O N
R A S U P P O S E D D Q
O U F E Q U A L L Y M U
P V D N L W K C P J N O
R I Q D J S U P P O R T
I N D O M I N A T E D A
A I V S E X I S T H P G
T S A C C E P T A B L E
E T H A R A S S M E N T
G E N E T I C A L L Y Y
```

There are 15 words from Unit 9 hidden in this puzzle. Can you find them? They are written either across, CAT, or down, C. The shortest word has five letters.
A
T

_____   _____

_____   _____

_____   _____

_____   _____

_____   _____

_____   _____

_____

H. Hidden message:

1	2	3	4		5	6	7	-	8	9	9	10	,																						
6		11	3	8		12	9	7	1	6	13	6	9	7	2	1		13	9		3	12	12	2	14	13		3		15	3	16	2	-	
1	9	15	6	7	3	13	2	1		11	9	4	10	6	7	17		2	7	18	6	4	9	7	15	2	7	13	.		15	19			
20	9	8	8		11	3		3		15	3	16	2		12	21	3	22	18	6	7	6	8	13		3	7	1							
13	21	2	4	2		11	2	4	2		7	9		9	14	14	9	4	13	22	7	6	13	6	2	8		23	9	4					
23(f)	2(e)	15(m)	3(a)	16(l)	2(e)		2	15	14	16	9	19	2	2	8	.		13	9		15	3	10	2		13	21	6	7	17	8			
11	9	4	8	2	,		15	19		20	9	8	8		11	3	8		15	19		21	22	8	20	3	7	1	.						
23	4	3	7	12	2	8	12	3																											

10. The Developing World

A. Fill in the blanks with a possible word:

1. The governments spend so much of the aid on their armed _____.

2. The bureaucracies are _____ with corruption.

3. The worst thing we can do is sit _____ and say they can't be solved.

4. They need to focus on _____ their economies.

5. Free _____ makes the rich richer.

6. A strong world economy _____ everybody.

7. The aid does more _____ than good.

8. _____ aid was rushed to the disaster victims.

9. _____ begins at home.

10. Something's better than _____.

B. Complete these sentences with your own ideas:

1. The best thing we can do to help developing countries is _____

2. I think developing countries should focus on _____

3. Countries that give aid _____

4. There's widespread poverty _____

5. I went through a hard time _____

C. Quiz:

1. Name a country that has refugee camps.   _____

2. Name a country that has a lot of debts.   _____

3. Name a multinational company.   _____

4. Name a registered charity.   _____

5. Name a country that spends too much on its armed forces.   _____

D. Jumbled up sentences:

1. poverty to government hunger the reduce does and little.
The _____

2. reducing countries corruption focus government developing on should.
Developing _____

3. their being trade protect countries industries prevents able free to from.
Free _____

4. much local their increase multinationals when factories too move salaries.
When _____

5. proceeds charity their go the album from will all latest to.
All _____

10. The Developing World

E. Sentences from words: *(write sentences that include these words)*

1. corruption

_____

2. refugee

_____

3. donate

_____

4. hunger

_____

5. appeal

_____

F. Writing dialogues: *(write at least an eight-line dialogue for each situation)*

1. Ask a charity worker about the problems in developing countries.

_____

_____

_____

_____

_____

_____

_____

_____

2. Talk about developing countries with the President of a multinational company.

_____

_____

_____

_____

_____

_____

_____

_____

_____

3. Talk with a friend about what you can both do to help developing countries.

____

____

____

____

____

____

____

____

G. Word search:

R	I	D	D	L	E	D	X	W	J	K	B
E	M	E	B	A	R	R	I	E	R	P	U
V	F	V	T	P	O	V	E	R	T	Y	R
I	B	E	P	P	J	P	F	B	D	P	E
T	K	L	R	E	F	U	G	E	E	K	A
A	D	O	N	A	T	E	M	N	F	H	U
L	S	P	F	L	K	B	L	E	C	U	C
I	N	I	G	N	O	R	E	F	W	N	R
Z	W	N	H	S	V	Q	J	I	L	G	A
I	M	G	C	H	A	R	I	T	Y	E	C
N	A	D	M	I	N	I	S	T	E	R	Y
G	C	O	R	R	U	P	T	I	O	N	J

There are 15 words from Unit 10 hidden in this puzzle. Can you find them? They are written either across, CAT, or down, C. The shortest word has six letters.
A
T

_______________ _______________

_______________ _______________

_______________ _______________

_______________ _______________

_______________ _______________

_______________ _______________

_______________ _______________

____

H. Hidden message:

1	2	3	4	■	5	3	6	7	8	9	,	■	■	■	■	■	■	■	■	■	■	■	■	■	■	■	■	■	■	■	■	■	■	■
8	7	■	5	3	6	10	■	21	2	7	21	16	2	■	3	4	2	■	1	10	11	6	12	■	13	4	7	5	■	■	■	■	■	■
9	14	6	12	2	4	■	7	4	■	3	4	2	■	11	6	■	6	2	2	1	■	7	13	■	3	11	1	.	■	11	15	■	■	■
8	7	5	2	15	11	5	2	8	■	8	2	2	5	8	■	15	9	3	15	■	16	11	15	15	16	2	■	7	13	■	17	9	3	15
17	2	■	1	7	6	3	15	2	■	3	18	15	14	3	16	16	10	■	12	2	15	8	■	15 t	9 h	4 r	7 o	14 u	12 g	9 h	■	15	7	■
15	9	7	8	2	■	17	9	7	■	6	2	2	1	■	11	15	.	■	19	14	15	■	2	20	2	4	10	■	16	11	15	15	16	2
19	11	15	■	9	2	16	21	8	.	■	17	2	■	9	3	20	2	■	15	7	■	22	2	2	21	■	15	4	10	11	6	12	.	■
3	19	2	6	3	■	■	■	■	■	■	■	■	■	■	■	■	■	■	■	■	■	■	■	■	■	■	■	■	■	■	■	■	■	■

11. Violence

A. Fill in the blanks with a possible word:

1. Violence has become a normal part of modern _____.

2. Victims are sometimes shot in cold _____.

3. In the past, people were _____ by aggression.

4. Movie stars are role _____ for young people.

5. There was less _____ of public property.

6. There's going to be a _____ amount of violence whatever we do.

7. If the media didn't _____ violence, there wouldn't be any problem.

8. We should only _____ to violence when there's no alternative.

9. I'm _____ to fight for what I believe in.

10. Mind your own _____!

B. Complete these sentences with your own ideas:

1. Sometimes criminals _____

2. There'd be less violent crime if _____

3. We should ban _____

4. The media is irresponsible when _____

5. Violence will escalate if _____

C. Quiz:

1. Name a violent criminal.   _____

2. Name something that was sensationalized by the media.   _____

3. Name somebody who's a good role model.   _____

4. Name a serial killer.   _____

5. Name somebody you hit it off with.   _____

D. Jumbled up sentences:

1. hostages we murders every taken news and day being of hear.
   Every _____

2. peaceful because we us so lives most it law-abiding violent find of live.
   We _____

3. and sports that out people all right message violent fight send hit a to it's.
   Violent _____

4. and as for sports aggression can war substitute act a.
   Sports _____

5. a rejects hands our we'll our on if have offer our boss fight.
   If _____

E. Sentences from words: *(write sentences that include these words)*

1. outlet

_____

2. revenge

_____

3. threaten

_____

4. irresponsible

_____

5. escalate

_____

F. Writing dialogues: *(write at least an eight-line dialogue for each situation)*

1. Interview a professional wrestler or boxer.

_____
_____
_____
_____
_____
_____
_____
_____

2. The police have caught you with a gun in a bank. Make excuses.

_____
_____
_____
_____
_____
_____
_____
_____

11. Violence

3. Talk with a news reporter who often writes sensational stories about famous people.

_____

_____

_____

_____

_____

_____

_____

Unit Assessment

G. Word search:

A	T	E	L	E	V	I	S	E	D	C	T
G	K	S	E	R	I	A	L	P	C	T	S
G	L	C	S	E	K	Z	H	L	O	H	U
R	N	A	P	V	I	C	T	I	M	R	B
E	J	L	W	E	V	N	S	W	M	E	S
S	B	A	N	N	E	D	K	M	I	A	T
S	B	T	J	G	T	M	T	C	T	T	I
I	F	I	Q	E	X	O	U	T	L	E	T
V	A	N	D	A	L	I	S	M	J	N	U
E	P	G	H	O	S	T	A	G	E	P	T
H	S	H	O	C	K	I	N	G	H	B	E
O	U	T	W	A	R	D	L	Y	G	F	V

There are 15 words from Unit 11 hidden in this puzzle. Can you find them? They are written either across, CAT, or down, C. The shortest word has six letters.
A
T

_____   _____

_____   _____

_____   _____

_____   _____

_____   _____

_____

H. Hidden message:

1	2	3	4		5	6	7	6	8	6	,																		
9	10	6	11	2	12	13	2		3	12	1		3	14	14	4	2	15	15	10	9	2		16	2	17	3	9	10	6	4
3	4	2		10	12	13	4	2	3	15	10	12	14		3	11	11		5	17	2		5	10	7	2	.		11	3	15	5
12	10	14	17	5		7	21		16	6	21	18	4	10	2	12	1		19	3	15		5	17	4	2	3	5	2	12	2	1
n	i	g	h	t																												
16	21		3		21	6	20	12	14		14	10	4	11	!		15	17	2		15	3	10	1		15	17	2		19	6	20	11	1
15	17	6	6	5		17	10	7		10	18		17	2		1	10	1	12	,	5		1	3	5	2		17	2	4	!		3	5
11	2	3	15	5			5	17	3	5	,	15		19	17	3	5		17	2		5	6	11	1		7	2	.				
13	17	4	10	15	5	10	12	3																								

12. Politics

A. Fill in the blanks with a possible word:

1. Politicians claim to _____ us.

2. Some politicians want power for its own _____.

3. Political campaigns require large _____ of money.

4. What would happen if radical _____ was necessary?

5. The system would lead to compromises on most _____ issues.

6. Your idea is rational but not _____ enough.

7. All men and women should be _____ to vote in the election.

8. The government's economic _____ isn't working.

9. We shouldn't talk about her behind her _____.

10. Some leaders try to take the _____ for others' hard work.

B. Complete these sentences with your own ideas:

1. Many politicians come across as _____

2. The politicians I generally trust _____

3. We need to radically change _____

4. When there's a major world crisis _____

5. My country's foreign policy _____

C. Quiz:

1. Name a moderate politician.   _____

2. Name a famous extremist.   _____

3. Name a right wing political party.   _____

4. Name a complacent politician.   _____

5. Name somebody who passes the buck.   _____

D. Jumbled up sentences:

1. different and seem both people wing so left ordinary politicians from right wing.
   Both _____

2. complacent parties corrupt when often become and comfortable political they are.
   When _____

3. would there long of was freedom as work speech it as.
   It _____

4. politicians deal able if major I the a crisis doubt would world to be with
   I _____

5. until the end campaign was go the recent touch very election and
   The _____

12. Politics

E. Sentences from words: *(write sentences that include these words)*

1. campaign

_____

2. majority

_____

3. corrupt

_____

4. bureaucrat

_____

5. policy

_____

F. Writing dialogues: *(write at least an eight-line dialogue for each situation)*

1. You want to be elected President or Prime Minister. Talk to a reporter.

_____

_____

_____

_____

_____

_____

_____

_____

2. Interview a corrupt politician.

_____

_____

_____

_____

_____

_____

_____

_____

_____

3. Talk with a politician who wants to increase taxes.

G. Word search:

C	O	M	P	R	O	M	I	S	E	K	M
O	I	A	M	B	I	T	I	O	N	R	O
M	D	N	J	C	O	N	S	U	M	E	D
P	E	C	A	M	P	A	I	G	N	P	E
L	O	D	Y	N	A	M	I	C	J	R	R
A	L	T	E	R	N	A	T	I	V	E	A
C	O	N	T	E	N	T	I	O	U	S	T
E	G	H	T	Z	P	H	N	L	W	E	E
N	Y	S	I	N	S	P	I	R	I	N	G
T	H	A	N	T	I	C	I	P	A	T	E
C	O	M	M	U	N	I	S	T	K	F	D
P	W	Z	E	X	T	R	E	M	I	S	T

There are 15 words from Unit 12 hidden in this puzzle. Can you find them? They are written either across, CAT, or down, C
A
T. The shortest word has seven letters.

H. Hidden message:

1	2	3	4		3	5	5	3	5	,																								
6	'	1		7	6	8	2		9	10		11	2		12 p	4 r	2 e	13 s	6 i	1 d	2 e	5 n	9 t	.		6	'	14		5	10	9		
7	2	15	9		10	4		4	6	16	17	9		18	6	5	16	.		6	'	14		5	10	9		3	5					
2	19	9	4	2	14	6	13	9		10	4		3	5		6	1	2	3	7	6	13	9	.		6	'	14		5	10	9		
2	20	2	5		3		14	10	1	2	4	3	9	2	.		6	5		15	3	21	9	,		6		17	3	20	2		5	10
13	9	4	10	5	16		12	10	7	6	9	6	21	3	7		10	12	6	5	6	10	5	13		3	9		3	7	7	.		
13	10		6		9	17	6	5	8		6	'	1		4	2	12	4	2	13	2	5	9		3		7	10	9		10	15		
12	2	10	12	7	2	.		9	10	14	10	8	10																					

13. Economics

A. Fill in the blanks with a possible word:

1. Economic _____ is stagnating.

2. If we increase exports, we'll reduce the trade _____.

3. If we increase productivity, the Gross National _____ should increase.

4. If everybody has more money _____ will increase.

5. The _____ effect may be negative, but the long-term effect should be positive.

6. Taxes on consumption are examples of _____ taxes.

7. The economy was booming but now it's in _____.

8. Entertaining clients is a good way to mix business with _____.

9. I paid too much tax so I should get a tax _____.

10. The end usually doesn't justify the _____.

B. Complete these sentences with your own ideas:

1. Inflation hurts _____

2. We can increase the productivity of a business by _____

3. Market research shows _____

4. If income tax is reduced _____

5. If I could take time off, I'd _____

C. Quiz:

1. Name a country with high inflation.   _____

2. Name a country that's in recession.   _____

3. Name a country with high income tax.   _____

4. Name one of your country's main exports.   _____

5. Name one of your country's main imports.   _____

D. Jumbled up sentences:

1. stimulate should so the growth productivity government economic as boost to.
The _____

2. market there's indicates for demand I've the products seen research our little.
The _____

3. economy rise term inflation improve but the slightly the may will long in.
The _____

4. rich income affect the progressive the poor more taxes than.
Progressive _____

5. you'll is worth of get the definitely tickets money's but price high your the.
The _____

E. Sentences from words: *(write sentences that include these words)*

1. production

_____

2. unemployment

_____

3. unprofitable

_____

4. revive

_____

5. objective

_____

F. Writing dialogues: *(write at least an eight-line dialogue for each situation)*

1. Discuss starting a business with a friend.

_____
_____
_____
_____
_____
_____
_____
_____
_____

2. Interview a successful businessman/woman.

_____
_____
_____
_____
_____
_____
_____
_____
_____

13. Economics

3. Talk with a friend about ways to improve your country's economy.

_____

_____

_____

_____

_____

_____

_____

_____

Unit Assessment

G. Word search:

U	N	E	M	P	L	O	Y	M	E	N	T
P	R	O	G	R	E	S	S	I	V	E	P
R	E	X	P	O	R	T	C	N	L	R	R
E	P	I	X	D	V	K	N	D	P	C	O
C	O	N	S	U	M	P	T	I	O	N	F
E	D	F	W	C	L	D	R	R	M	M	I
S	E	L	S	T	R	A	D	E	K	A	T
S	F	A	N	I	J	F	C	C	P	R	A
I	I	T	L	V	L	S	D	T	W	K	B
O	C	I	B	I	R	E	B	A	T	E	L
N	I	O	S	T	I	M	U	L	A	T	E
D	T	N	C	Y	F	A	C	T	O	R	S

There are 15 words from Unit 13 hidden in this puzzle. Can you find them? They are written either across, CAT, or down, C. The shortest word has five letters.
A
T

_____   _____

_____   _____

_____   _____

_____   _____

_____   _____

_____   _____

_____

H. Hidden message:

1	2	3	4		5	6	7	-	8	9	9	10 ,																	
6	11		12	9	7	8	13	14	15	16	6	9	7		6	7	12	4	2	3	8	2	8 ,		6	16	17	6	18	18
19	9	9	8	16		2	12	9	7	9	14	6	12		20 g	4 r	9 o	17 w	16 t	21 h		3	7	1	4	2	1	13	12	2
16	21	2		16	4	3	1	2		1	2	11	6	12	6	16 .			16	21	2		20	9	22	2	4	7	14	2	7	16
17	6	18	18		16	21	2	7		6	7	12	4	2	3	8	2		16	3	23		16	9		15	4	2	22	2	7	16
6	7	11	18	3	16	6	9	7 ,		8	9		2	9	7	8	13	14	15	16	6	9	7		17	6	18	18
1	2	12	4	2	3	8	2		17 ,		18	18		19	2		3	12	12	10		17	21	2	4	2		17	2
8	16	3	4	16	2	1 .		7	3	24	6	14

14. Happiness

A. Fill in the blanks with a possible word:

1. I don't go _____ for opportunities.

2. I don't feel deeply _____ by anything.

3. I _____ the best of my situation.

4. I can think of _____ better than to be on a romantic island.

5. I could _____ a happy family.

6. I want to try to improve society as a _____.

7. My job's OK for the time _____.

8. I have a very happy _____ of our vacation together in Greece.

9. I'm in a _____ mood. Here's $10,000.

10. A _____ is as good as a rest.

B. Complete these sentences with your own ideas:

1. I tend to complain about _____

2. One of my goals in life is to _____

3. I find it difficult to think positively when _____

4. I feel inhibited when _____

5. I'm completely satisfied with _____

C. Quiz:

1. Name somebody who's very calm.   _____

2. Name a fulfilling occupation.   _____

3. Name a story with a happy ending.   _____

4. Name somebody who's often in a playful mood.   _____

5. Name somebody you think is too self-satisfied.   _____

D. Jumbled up sentences:

1. satisfied doesn't does deeply by he he feel anything.
He _____

2. get telling only I things better myself keep can.
I _____

3. a happiness to my island idea romantic is on of live.
My _____

4. world living the those us too of immediate concerned around ways with are.
Those _____

5. moving mixed York I away feelings New have from about.
I _____

14. Happiness

Unit Assessment

E. Sentences from words: *(write sentences that include these words)*

1. achievement

_____

2. surrounded

_____

3. purpose

_____

4. mood

_____

5. blissfully

_____

F. Writing dialogues: *(write at least an eight-line dialogue for each situation)*

1. Talk with a friend about things that make you unhappy.

_____
_____
_____
_____
_____
_____
_____
_____

2. Interview a movie star or pop star who is very unhappy.

_____
_____
_____
_____
_____
_____
_____
_____

3. Complain to your teacher about your English lessons.

_____

_____

_____

_____

_____

_____

_____

G. Word search:

I	M	M	E	D	I	A	T	E	K	W	Q
N	P	C	C	O	N	C	E	R	N	E	D
H	A	O	H	J	C	H	H	R	W	B	F
I	R	M	S	A	T	I	S	F	I	E	D
B	A	P	D	Q	S	E	N	S	E	S	M
I	D	L	T	W	Q	V	N	X	U	M	E
T	I	A	D	I	R	E	C	T	I	O	N
E	S	I	G	Y	L	M	F	B	K	O	D
D	E	N	F	O	R	E	V	E	R	D	I
S	U	R	R	O	U	N	D	E	D	J	N
W	S	I	T	U	A	T	I	O	N	N	G
F	U	L	F	I	L	L	I	N	G	F	I

There are 15 words from Unit 14 hidden in this puzzle. Can you find them? They are written either across, CAT, or down, C. The shortest word has four letters.
A
T

_____   _____

_____   _____

_____   _____

_____   _____

_____   _____

_____   _____

_____

H. Hidden message:

1	2	3	4		3	5	2	6	3	,															
7	8		9	10	4	11		12	13		14	15	16	14	12	16	16	12	6	17	,		12		18	19	12	6	11
20	10	13	12	18	12	21	2	16	8		3	6	1		7	3	11	2		18	19	2		7	10	13	18		10	14
2	21	2	4	8		10	20	20	10	4	18	15	6	12	18	8		18	19	3	18		22	10	7	2	13		7	8
9	3	8	,		3	6	1		12	,	7		1	2	2	20	16	8		13	3	18	12	13	14	12	2	1		5	8
7	8		20	2	4	13	10	6	3	16		16	12	14	2			5	15	18		12	,	7		21	2	4	8
			p	e	r	s	o	n	a	l					.														
15	6	19	3	20	20	8	.		12		19	3	21	2		6	10		7	10	4	2		17	10	3	16	13		12	6
16	12	14	2	.		22	19	2	6																				

15. Globalization

A. Fill in the blanks with a possible word:

1. More people are developing an international _____.

2. People in the cities have more cosmopolitan _____ of thinking.

3. Even the most well-_____ experts seem prejudiced.

4. I've had itchy _____ ever since I first went overseas.

5. I often _____ into people who have never seen a kangaroo.

6. Some people come _____ as being uninternational.

7. Education is the _____ to making our society more international.

8. We need to look at things from many points of _____.

9. In a _____ world everybody would be rich and happy.

10. It takes all _____ to make a world.

B. Complete these sentences with your own ideas:

1. People from different racial backgrounds _____

2. Ethnic minorities often _____

3. I would be more international if _____

4. Multi-racial communities tend to _____

5. I think the global coverage of _____

C. Quiz:

1. Name a relatively homogeneous society.   _____

2. Name a cosmopolitan city.   _____

3. Name a common prejudice in your society.   _____

4. Name a nationalistic politician.   _____

5. Name somebody who often travels from place to place.   _____

D. Jumbled up sentences:

1. standardized are perspectives some suppressed cultures global being by.
Some _____

2. on opinions stereotypes seem and even based experts' be prejudice to often.
Even _____

3. traveling everybody place I'm me to the got grateful in who first in interested.
I'm _____

4. very who across some traveled have international people being come never as.
Some _____

5. to to potential we order question full need our in reach fundamentals.
We _____

E. Sentences from words: *(write sentences that include these words)*

1. melting

_____

2. straightforward

_____

3. dampen

_____

4. open-minded

_____

5. apparently

_____

F. Writing dialogues: *(write at least an eight-line dialogue for each situation)*

1. Explain to a visitor about one of your local customs or festivals.

_____
_____
_____
_____
_____
_____
_____
_____

2. Talk with a friend about a trip you took to another country.

_____
_____
_____
_____
_____
_____
_____
_____

15. Globalization

3. Interview a member of an ethnic minority about the prejudice he/she has experienced.

_____

_____

_____

_____

_____

_____

_____

_____

Unit Assessment

G. Word search:

C	O	S	M	O	P	O	L	I	T	A	N
O	U	T	L	O	O	K	V	D	G	D	T
M	M	E	L	V	T	D	R	A	I	V	F
M	E	R	I	X	E	Q	P	M	M	A	L
U	L	E	T	H	N	I	C	P	P	N	E
N	T	O	C	M	T	F	Z	E	R	T	X
I	I	T	H	W	I	N	U	N	E	A	I
T	N	Y	Y	R	A	F	D	S	S	G	B
Y	G	P	H	R	L	K	V	B	S	E	L
W	P	E	R	S	P	E	C	T	I	V	E
Q	H	O	M	O	G	E	N	E	O	U	S
P	B	A	C	K	G	R	O	U	N	D	J

There are 15 words from Unit 15 hidden in this puzzle. Can you find them? They are written either across, CAT, or down, C. The shortest word has five letters.
A
T

_____   _____

_____   _____

_____   _____

_____   _____

_____   _____

_____   _____

_____

H. Hidden message:

1	2	3	4		5	4	3	6	7	2	8	7	3	,	

| 9 | | 10 | 9 | 11 | 2 | | 9 | 6 | | 3 | | 12 | 13 | 10 | 14 | 9 | – | 4 | 3 | 7 | 9 | 3 | 10 |

| 7 | 15 | 8 | 12 | 15 | 16 | 15 | 10 | 9 | 14 | 3 | 6 | | 7 | 9 | 14 | 17 | | 18 | 19 | 2 | 4 | 2 | | 2 | 14 | 19 | 6 | 9 | 7 |

| 12 | 9 | 6 | 15 | 4 | 9 | 14 | 9 | 2 | 8 | | 3 | 4 | 2 | | 14 | 15 | 10 | 2 | 4 | 3 | 14 | 2 | 1 | | 3 | 6 | 1 | | 12 | 15 | 8 | 14 |

| 16 | 2 | 15 | 16 | 10 | 2 | | 19 | 3 | 11 | 2 | | 3 | 6 | | 9 | 6 | 14 | 2 | 4 | 6 | 3 | 14 | 9 | 15 | 6 | 3 | 10 |

| 15 | 13 | 14 | 10 | 15 | 15 | 20 | . | | 21 | 13 | 14 | , | | 16 | 2 | 4 | 8 | 15 | 6 | 3 | 10 | 10 | 17 | | 9 | | 19 | 3 | 11 | 2 |
| o | u | t | l | o | o | k |

| 12 | 3 | 6 | 17 | | 16 | 4 | 2 | 22 | 13 | 7 | 9 | 7 | 2 | 8 | . | | 9 | | 23 | 13 | 2 | 8 | 8 | | 9 | 14 | | 14 | 3 | 20 | 2 | 8 |

| 3 | 10 | 10 | | 8 | 15 | 4 | 14 | 8 | | 14 | 15 | | 12 | 3 | 20 | 2 | | 3 | | 18 | 15 | 4 | 10 | 1 | . | | 7 | 3 | 4 | 10 | 15 | 8 |

Oral Interview Questions

Unit 1

1. Talk about whether you tend to be optimistic or pessimistic.

2. Talk about whether you tend to be decisive or indecisive.

3. Talk about your attitude towards international marriages.

4. Talk about whether or not you have prejudices.

5. You are a psychiatrist. Try to find out why I'm bad-tempered.

Unit 2

1. Talk about what you would do if you had a lot of money.

2. Talk about how your character might change if you had a lot of money.

3. Talk about we should all get paid the same amount of money.

4. Talk about whether you think competition in society is good or bad.

5. You want to sell your business to me. Persuade me to buy it.

Unit 3

1. Talk about how you could take better care of your health.

2. Talk about whether you think medical care should be free.

3. Talk about an injury or sickness you have had.

4. Talk about whether you could be a good doctor.

5. You are a doctor. Try to find out what's wrong with me.

Unit 4

1. Talk about your favorite subjects at school.

2. Talk about the qualities of a good teacher.

3. Talk about how to motivate students to learn.

4. Talk about whether tests have a positive effect on learning.

5. Try to find out my opinions on how to teach effectively.

Unit 5

1. Talk about how the amount of crime can be reduced.

2. Talk about whether you think the death penalty is necessary.

3. Talk about any rules or laws you have broken.

4. Talk about why some people become criminals.

5. You are a policeman/woman who suspects I robbed a bank.

Oral Interview Questions

Unit 6

1. Talk about the effects of global warming.

2. Talk about how we can protect the environment better.

3. Talk about a place you know that has a very good natural environment.

4. Talk about how long you think the human race will survive.

5. I am the President of the USA. Try to persuade me to do more for the environment.

Unit 7

1. Talk about whether or not aliens have visited the Earth.

2. Talk about what we will find if we travel into outer space.

3. Talk about what you would do if you found your best friend was an alien.

4. Talk about whether it's important to spend a lot of money on space exploration.

5. I'm an alien who's just arrived on Earth. Interview me.

Unit 8

1. Talk about the period in history you are most interested in.

2. Talk about a person in history you admire.

3. Talk about lessons we can learn from history.

4. Talk about what you will be able to do when you can speak English fluently.

5. I'm a famous historical figure. Interview me.

Unit 9

1. Talk about how women suffer from discrimination at work.

2. Talk about the best ways to achieve more equality between men and women.

3. Talk about how women may be conditioned to accept inferior roles.

4. Talk about how you like men to treat women.

5. Interview me for a job that is normally done by a member of the opposite sex.

Unit 10

1. Talk about how rich countries can help developing countries more.

2. Talk about the reasons why some countries are richer than others.

3. Talk about whether multinational companies have a positive or negative influence.

4. Talk about policies governments of developing countries should focus on.

5. Your country has much poverty, and I want to build a factory there. Interview me.

Unit 11

1. Talk about the effect of violent sports on society.

2. Talk about whether the media sensationalizes violence.

3. Talk about whether society is becoming more or less violent.

4. Talk about whether you would fight for your country.

5. I'm a dangerous criminal who's just about to shoot you. Persuade me not to.

Unit 12

1. Talk about the political situation in your country.

2. Talk about a politician you respect (past or present).

3. Talk about how there can be more freedom in the world.

4. Talk about your ideal political system.

5. You want to be Mayor of your town/city. Persuade me to vote for you.

Unit 13

1. Talk about the current economic situation in your country.

2. Talk about which taxes should be increased and which decreased.

3. Talk about other economic measures your government needs to take.

4. Talk about future trends in the world economy.

5. I want to start a business. Give me advice.

Unit 14

1. Talk about a time when you are blissfully happy.

2. Talk about your dream lifestyle.

3. Talk about whether or not you make the most of opportunities.

4. Talk about whether your life has a purpose, and what it is.

5. Complain to me about the things in your life you dislike most.

Unit 15

1. Talk about how the world can become more peaceful.

2. Talk about how we can educate children to have more international minds.

3. Talk about how racial prejudice can be reduced.

4. Talk about popular images of your country that you feel are inaccurate.

5. Tell me about the characteristics of people and society in your country that you feel are important.

1. Attitudes

Francesca: Maybe I'm *paranoid/negative/pessimistic*. Whenever I'm in a serious relationship, I always think my boyfriend is playing around with other girls. I have these deep emotional fears, even if I know he's at home reading a book! I'd probably better see a *psychiatrist*.

Chen: That's surprising. You always seem so *optimistic/positive/easygoing/tolerant* and *optimistic/ positive/easygoing/tolerant*, so I've always imagined that you trust people without hesitation.

Francesca: Yes, everybody seems to see me as a *positive/easygoing/tolerant* person who is always smiling and in a good mood, but in reality I'm about as *pessimistic/paranoid/narrow-minded/negative* as they come, and I can't tolerate any of my boyfriend's flirting – real or imagined!

2. Money

Christina: I have some money that I'd like to *invest/deposit*, but I'm not sure what to do with it. There's no point in just leaving it in the bank. It wouldn't *earn* much *interest*.

Manosh: You could study the *stock market* and buy some shares in a company that's doing well, but it can be risky. There's no guarantee that the *value* of the shares will increase, so you run the risk of losing much of your money.

Christina: Yes, I might make a *loss*. Perhaps the safest way is to buy a new house or start my own small business. I could use my savings for the initial *deposit* for the house or as starting *capital* for the business.

3. Health

Tomoko: I played tennis yesterday, and my legs are very *sore/stiff/swollen* and *sore/stiff/swollen* today. I can hardly walk. It's not a sports *injury* or anything like that. I just usually don't take enough exercise, so my body *aches* all over.

Nazim: I know how you feel. Exercise can sometimes do more harm than good! But, don't worry! I have some great *medicine/ointments* that will clear everything up in no time. You just rub it into your *stiff/sore* muscles a couple of times a day.

Tomoko: Thank you for the offer, but I think I'll see a doctor. I have a lot of allergies, and if I'm not careful I could easily get a *rash* all over my legs. It's incredible how even very common creams and *ointments/medicine* can have serious *side effects*.

4. Education

Carlos: I only went to *single-sex* schools. There were no girls at all. It was so unnatural! And the style of teaching was so old-fashioned! The *curriculum* wasn't flexible at all. All *subjects* were *compulsory* until we were seventeen, and then we could make a few choices.

Annan: I bet you studied many *subjects* that I'll never get a chance to know much about. At the schools I went to, we had a lot of freedom of choice, but I often wonder if we learned enough. One very good thing was that lessons tended to be *student-centered*, so most of us were motivated to study at home by ourselves.

Carlos: That's great! Your teachers obviously understood the importance of self-*motivation*. We just followed *rules* and did what we were told. There was nothing to entice us to study for ourselves. And the strictness and hierarchy led to a lot of *bullying* as well.

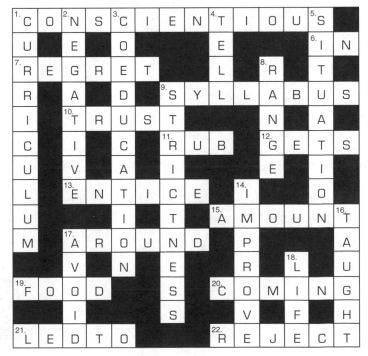

5. Crime

Manosh: I was *arrested* once. I was *innocent*, of course. I didn't do anything illegal, but a *witness* identified me through a computer search, and I had no alibi, so I was *suspected/arrested* by the police. It was an absurd situation. I had no connection with the crime at all, and no *motive* to commit it.

Jin-Sook: That must have been a terrible experience. Was there a *trial*? Did you have to appear in *court*? Were you *sentenced/convicted*? I suppose everything turned out OK in the end. It must have done, or you wouldn't be here now.

Manosh: Fortunately, it never went to *court*. If I'd been prosecuted and found guilty, I could have been *sentenced* to a few years in prison. But I was branded as a *criminal* for a few months. Even some of my best friends began to doubt me, and I had to change jobs because of all the *suspicion* around me at work.

Crossword grid (Crime):

1.D	E	2.E	P	R	3.O	O	4.T	E	D		5.N
E		F			W		I				6.T	H	A	T
7.L	I	F	E		8.N	U	M	B	E	R		R		
I		E				E			R		I		R	
9.B	E	C	O	M	E	10.M					A		O	
E		T				O		11.F	O	L	L	O	W	12.S
R						T	13.C						E
14.A	L	15.I	B	I			H			16.S		17.A	T
T		M		V		18.A	C	C	U	S	E	D	
19.E	X	P	L	A	I	N				P		V
L		R			T		C			R		20.H	I	T
Y	21.E	V	I	D	E	N	C	E					C
	S			S	O				22.M	O	N	E	Y
23.S	E	N	T	E	N	C	E		

6. The Environment

Abena: The weather is completely different from what it was like twenty years ago. I'm sure it's all because of *global warming* caused by the *greenhouse effect*. It's frightening.

Chen: So many of these problems are simply the side effects of industrialization, consumerism, and exploitation of poorer countries. It's probably too late to do anything. Even if we cut down on carbon dioxide *emissions* and replant the *rain forests*, it won't make much difference.

Abena: I hope you aren't right, but it does look like we may have permanently destroyed the Earth's *ecosystem* in so many ways. To stand any chance at all, we have to stop using *pesticides/toxic chemicals* and *pesticides/toxic chemicals*, stop polluting the air and water, and radically change our way of life.

Crossword grid (The Environment):

1.O		2.O	B	V	3.I	O	U	4.S	L	Y		5.G
R		Z			L			I				R
6.G	L	O	B	A	7.L			8.D	A	M	9.A	G	E
A		N		10.S	E	R	V	E			D		E
11.N	E	E	12.D		G			13.R	A	I	N
I			14.E	X	A	15.M		16.P			P		H
17.C	18.A	S	E			19.L	I	F	E				O
	L		P			I		S		20.S			U
21.A	L	L		22.A	N	D		23.T	R	U	S	T	S
	E			I					I		B		E
24.B	R	A	25.N	D	E	D			C		26.J	O	27.B
G			O					I		E		A
I			28.W			M	E	D	I	C	I	N	E
C			N			E			E		T		K

7. Aliens

Nazim: I wonder if people will ever be able to travel to other *galaxies*. Rockets will need to travel faster than the *speed of light*, *astronomers* will have to identify planets that can support human life, and there'll be many other problems to overcome. I wonder if it will ever happen.

Annan: There have been many *sightings* of *UFOs/flying saucers* that seem to have come from *outer space*. So, if aliens can visit us, I expect we'll be able to visit their planets one day.

Nazim: I know it must sound like I read too much *science fiction*, but maybe we'll discover some completely new technology that enables us to travel through *black holes* or shift into another *dimension* so as to cover distances much faster.

8. History

Francesca: I wish I could have lived during the *Renaissance*. It would have been wonderful to see the old ways of the *medieval period*, such as the *feudal system*, being challenged and reformed. I might even have met a great artist like Michelangelo or Leonardo da Vinci!

Carlos: The reality was probably pretty horrible. There may have been a lot of *innovation/reform* going on around you, but you probably would have been sick most of the time unless, perhaps, you were a member of the *aristocracy*, and even then you would have been constantly caught up in wars with other countries or in some *civil war*.

Francesca: I guess it wasn't until the *Industrial Revolution* that modern society developed, and even that was paid for by suffering in factories in the industrializing countries, and by the exploitation of people in *colonies*. So, despite the problems we have today, at least we live healthier and happier lives.

9. Women in Society

Tomoko: Our society is so *male-dominated*. People talk about *equal opportunities*, but, in fact, men have all the power. In many jobs, they can even get away with *sexual harassment* of female employees, and all kinds of *sexist* comments.

Chen: I think that's partly because some women want to have *careers* in occupations more suited to men. We should accept that we are *genetically* different. There is very little *discrimination/sexual harassment* in jobs that are more *appropriate* for women.

Tomoko: How can you say that! Even in most of those jobs, a higher percentage of managers are men. And the jobs you imagine are more *appropriate* for men only appear so because of *social customs* created by men. We need *affirmative action* to ensure there's a *quota* of female managers in all major companies.

```
 1.A  C  C  E  P  T  ▓ 4.T  ▓ 5.T  ▓  ▓ 6.G
   F  ▓ 2.O  ▓  ▓  ▓ 7.O  U  R  S  E  L  V  E  S
 8.F  E  U  D  A  L  ▓  E  ▓  L  ▓  ▓  T
   I  ▓  R  ▓ 9.E  N  A  B  L  E  ▓ 10.I
11.R  I  S  K  ▓  R  ▓  T  ▓  I  ▓ 12.R  U  N
   M  ▓  E  ▓  A  ▓  ▓  N  ▓  ▓  G
   A  ▓  ▓  ▓ 13.T 14.H  I  N  G 15.S  ▓  R
16.T  O  N  G  U  E  ▓  N  ▓  O  ▓  E
   I  ▓ 17.A  ▓  ▓  N  ▓ 18.U  S  E  D
   V  ▓  T  ▓ 19.P  O  P  U  L  A  R  ▓  I
20.E  Q  U  A  L  ▓  E  ▓  C  ▓  E
   ▓  R  ▓ 21.A  M  O  N  G  ▓ 22.E 23.A  R  N
   ▓  A  ▓  C  ▓  D  ▓  ▓  I  ▓  T
24.P  O  L  L  E  N  ▓ 25.O  U  T  E  R  ▓  S
```

10. The Developing World

Francesca: What's the point of *donating aid/charity* to developing countries? The governments spend so much of it on their *armed forces* and do very little to reduce *hunger/poverty/corruption/debts* and *hunger/poverty/corruption/debts*. And the government bureaucracies that administer the *aid/charity* are riddled with *corruption/debts*.

Christina: There are many people in developing countries and at the *United Nations* who are trying to fight these problems. The worst thing we can do is sit back and say problems like *hunger/poverty/corruption/debts* and *hunger/poverty/corruption/debts* cannot be solved, or ignore all the people in *refugee* camps who need our help.

Francesca: I think developing countries should first focus on *birth control/refugee* programs, reducing government *corruption/debts*, and revitalizing their economies. Then we can consider *aid/charity* and *aid/charity*.

```
 1.B  A 2.R  R  I  E  R  ▓ 3.D  ▓ 4.T  ▓ 5.D
   U  ▓  E  ▓  ▓  ▓ 6.P  O  V  E  R  T  Y
   R  ▓  F  ▓ 7.P  ▓  N  ▓  ▓  A  ▓  N
 8.E  Q  U  A  L  L  Y  ▓ 9.A  C  I  D  ▓  A
   A  ▓  G  ▓  A  ▓  T  ▓  E  ▓  M
   U  ▓  E  ▓ 10.A  N  C  I  E  N  T  ▓  I
11.C  R  E 12.A  T  E  ▓  ▓  ▓  ▓  C
   R  ▓  T  ▓  T  ▓ 13.S 14.P  O  R  T 15.S
   A  ▓  T  ▓ 16.D  O  ▓  E
17.C  I  V  I  L  ▓ 18.E  X  I  S 19.T  R
   Y  ▓  T  ▓  B  ▓  N  ▓  R  ▓  I
   ▓ 20.T  R  U  E  ▓  T  ▓ 21.T  R  E  M  O  R
   O  ▓  D  ▓  ▓  ▓  I  ▓  E  ▓  U
22.H  O  N  E  Y  M  O  O  N  S  ▓  S
```

11. Violence

Annan: Violence has become a normal part of modern society. Every day we hear news of murders, *terrorism/vandalism*, *hostages* being taken … Sometimes criminals single out innocent *victims* and shoot them in cold blood. Even children commit these kinds of horrible crimes.

Nazim: It's certainly true that we live in a very *aggressive* world, but don't you think we find it so *shocking* because most of us live peaceful, law-abiding lives? In the past, people were surrounded by aggression and war, but, these days, most of us just watch it on TV.

Annan: The situation may have got better before it got worse. When I was a child, I could walk the streets around my house at night, and the TV and movie stars who were *role models* for young people were not so outwardly *aggressive*, and there was less *vandalism* of public property.

12. Politics

Manosh: I can't understand what politicians really want in life. Both conservative and *socialist/left wing/moderate/extremist* politicians seem so different from ordinary people, even though they claim to *represent* us. Are they genuine *idealists*, or do they just want power for its own sake and dream of becoming *Prime Minister* or President some day?

Nazim: It must depend on the person. I generally trust *left wing* politicians more than *right wing* ones, but even many socialists or communists come across as insincere and consumed by ambition.

Manosh: I guess that's why *interest groups* have so much influence. We're supposed to live in a democracy, but, in fact, for a political candidate to win a *majority* in an *election*, he or she has to manipulate people's opinions through a *campaign* that requires large sums of money supplied by *interest groups*. That's hardly democratic!

13. Economics

Carlos: The economy's in a mess. The *trade deficit* is getting larger, *productivity/consumption/economic growth* is declining, and *productivity/consumption/economic growth* is stagnating. If things get any worse, we'll be in *recession*.

Manosh: The government should do something. They always talk about the need for new, progressive ideas, and radical action, but it's just talk. They should encourage *exports* so as to reduce the *trade deficit*, and boost *consumption/productivity* so as to stimulate *economic growth*.

Carlos: They are always too cautious, and so afraid of *inflation*. All the *market research* that I've ever seen indicates that there's no serious danger of prices increasing too fast. We have to focus on avoiding *recession*.

14. Happiness

Chen: I don't know if I'm happy or not. I certainly try to *make the most of* the opportunities that come my way, but I don't really have a clear *goal* in life, and don't go looking for opportunities. I guess I'm too *inhibited*, so I *miss out on* a lot of things. How about you? Are you happy?

Abena: Well, I find it easy to stay *calm*, and I'm usually in a good *mood*, so I guess I'm reasonably happy. When it comes down to it, I don't have a lot to *complain* about. However, I don't feel deeply *satisfied* by anything I do. I'm still looking for something *fulfilling*.

Chen: Speaking very frankly, my job's boring, I can't find a girlfriend, and I don't have much money, but I *make the best of* my situation and try to *think positively*. I always tell myself that things can only get better.

15. Globalization

Abena: Exposure to the world through information provided by the *global* media may be leading to the false impression that more people are developing an international *outlook*, whereas, in fact, it may be making many people less *open-minded/cosmopolitan*.

Nazim: I can see that members of *ethnic minorities* may feel their cultures are being suppressed by standardized *global perspectives*. This may be particularly true in *homogeneous* areas rather than *multi-racial/heterogeneous* ones. In the larger cities, I think people have more *cosmopolitan/open-minded* ways of thinking.

Abena: I'm not convinced that the larger *cosmopolitan/multi-racial* cities are the *melting pots* they are supposed to be. Things may be worse when people from different racial and ethnic *backgrounds* live side by side. Even the most well-informed experts in these apparently *cosmopolitan/open-minded* cities often express opinions that seem to be based on prejudice and *stereotypes*.

1.C	O	2.N	V	3.I	N	4.C	E	5.D			6.V	
O		O		M		O		7.E	T	8.H	N	I	C
N		T		M		M		S		A		C	
9.S	T	A	T	E	M	E	N	T		R		T	
U		B		D				10.R	E	M	A	I	N
11.M	E	L	T	I	N	12.G		O				M	
P		E		A		13.A	N	Y			14.P		15.S
T				T		R					R		U
16.I	C	E	17.B	E	R	G		18.A	C	R	O	S	S
O			R			L		P			D		P
N		19.M	I	X		20.E	X	P	O	S	U	R	E
	21.T		G			E		E			C		C
	O		22.H	23.A	B	I	T	24.A	T		T		T
25.S	O	R	T	S				26.L	O	S	S	E	S

Student's Book Answers • 113

Teacher's Book Answers

The students may come up with alternative answers that are also possible. These should be encouraged and accepted.

UNIT 1

Listening/Reading Worksheet

B
1. time　　　2. true　　　3. help
4. look

D
attitude, communicate, experience, similar, way, impossible, negative

E
1. 5: pessimistic, probably, problems, positive, parents
2. I can't help/it seems impossible/I can't change.
3. similar to
4. completely, never
5. international

F
1. She's sure that she will always argue with her foreign boyfriend.
2. She can't change the way she feels.
3. A more international environment.

G
1. She wishes she could find a way to be with him.
2. He thinks she should go into her marriage with a positive attitude.
3. He thinks she should take a close look at the reasons for her attitudes.

H
1. Finding a way to live with her boyfriend.
3. If she married someone more similar to herself.
5. The way she feels.

Unit Assessment

A
1. fears　　　2. pessimistic　　　3. paranoid

4. sad　　　5. way　　　6. into
7. thinking　　8. rooted　　9. going
10. less

D
1. I've always imagined she believes people without hesitation.
2. Everybody seems to see me as a broad-minded person.
3. We can't help the way we feel.
4. I wish I could find a way to change my attitude.
5. My new boss gets on my nerves.

G
Word search
tolerant, paranoid, decisive, optimistic, similar, lateral, patronizing, prejudice, attitude, attention, easygoing, arguments, communicate, experience, negative

H
Hidden message
Dear Tomoko,
Your attitude seems so narrow-minded! Why are you so prejudiced against marrying a foreigner? I think you need to be much more tolerant and positive, and just marry your boyfriend if you love him! Jin-Sook.

UNIT 2

Listening/Reading Worksheet

B
1. paid　　　2. work　　　3. value
4. point

D
value, amount, incentive, focus, sense, nature

E
1. 12: selfishness, stress, should, same, some, spend, simple, society, social, sense, suffers, so
2. received
3. missing the point
4. in
5. tend, about

F

1. People could choose what to spend their money on.
2. People wouldn't work hard.
3. We forget about other work incentives.

G

1. It makes us greedy and competitive.
2. We need competition to encourage us to improve society.
3. They work hard because they like the people they are working with.

H

1. Money makes us greedy.
3. It encourages us to develop and improve society.
5. They believe in the social value of what they are doing.

Unit Assessment

A

1. interest	2. risk	3. paid
4. nature	5. value	6. quality
7. point	8. raise	9. price
10. rainy		

D

1. There's no point in leaving it in the bank.
2. If we all got the same amount, many people wouldn't work hard.
3. Some people work hard out of a sense of responsibility.
4. The net profit will be a lot less than the gross profit.
5. I think most people are finding things tough.

G

Word search
greedy, incentive, amount, deposit, profit, business, competitive, focus, basically, interest, margin, waste, worth, capital, invest

H

Hidden message
Dear Manosh,
We are making a profit at the moment, but not

enough to risk investing in the stock market. It would just be a waste of money. It doesn't grow on trees, you know! I think wc should just save it for a rainy day. Francesca

UNIT 3

Listening/Reading Worksheet

B

1. right	2. give	3. prescribe
4. pay		

D

medicine, prescribe, dynamic, surgeries, treatment, toes, forces

E

1. 14: poor, possible, play, part, practice, patients, private, prescribe, poorer, problems, provided, people, pay, provide
2. make money
3. in practice
4. health care
5. civil servants

F

1. Because health care is a basic human right.
2. Market forces are effective in keeping doctors on their toes.
3. Patients who are not really sick.

G

1. Health care is a basic human right.
2. Doctors sometimes refuse to give unnecessary treatment.
3. Paying too much tax reduces incentives.

H

1. Money should play no part in deciding who gets medical treatment.
3. Market forces can be effective in keeping doctors on their toes.
5. Medical care is sometimes provided by governments.

Teacher's Book Answers

Unit assessment

A

1. aches	2. harm	3. time
4. rash	5. right	6. practice
7. applied	8. provide	9. neglects
10. slip		

D

1. Even the most common creams and ointments can have serious side effects.
2. Market forces can be effective in keeping doctors on their toes.
3. If a doctor refuses to give unnecessary treatment, the patient will change doctors.
4. Taxes to support old people make the economy less dynamic.
5. Your arguments just go in one ear and out the other.

G

Word search

medicine, insurance, injury, prescribe, treatment, allergies, according, provide, patient, neglect, emergency, exercise, swollen, surgeries, unnecessary

H

Hidden message

Dear Christina,
I have a sore throat, a stiff neck, a swollen knee, a rash all down my back, and my stomach aches. I know I need to go to a hospital and receive treatment. But I can't. I'm allergic to doctors. They make me feel sick. Tomoko

UNIT 4

Listening/Reading Worksheet

B

1. up	2. through	3. do
4. exactly		

D

graduate, explaining, curiosity, exactly, syllabus

E

1. 4: chance, choose, curiosity, creativity
2. find things out
3. through
4. telling me what to do
5. exactly, way

F

1. She wants to find things out for herself.
2. To help the teacher get through the syllabus.
3. Because the school system destroys their curiosity and creativity.

G

1. Teachers should stop telling students what to do.
2. Teachers need time to get through the syllabus.
3. The school system destroys students' curiosity and creativity.

H

1. They will have time to choose the things they want to learn.
3. music, bikes, sport
5. The way she has been taught.

Unit assessment

A

1. single-sex	2. motivated	3. entice
4. herself	5. through	6. way
7. all	8. qualified	9. head
10. experience		

D

1. I often wonder if we learned very much.
2. Most of them were motivated to study by themselves at home.
3. The strictness and hierarchy led to a lot of bullying.
4. All they have to do is stop explaining.
5. The school system destroys our curiosity and creativity.

G

Word search

curriculum, compulsory, motivation, syllabus, memorize, discover, curiosity, graduate, exactly, creativity, qualified, centered, subject, bullying, strictness

H

Hidden message
Dear Abena,
I wonder if our teacher's qualified. His lessons are way over our heads, and I don't think he's following a syllabus. And the other day he even asked for all our telephone numbers. This is a single-sex, girls' school! Jin-Sook

UNIT 5

Listening/Reading Worksheet

B

1. less   2. show   3. sentencing
4. example

D

heat, innocent, consequences, consideration, noticeable

E

1. 12: should, somebody, show, some, states, seem, spend, society, sentencing, says, sometimes, setting
2. evidence
3. important
4. deliberately
5. innocent

F

1. They don't consider the consequences of their actions.
2. They may kill more innocent people.
3. It sends a message that violence and killing are ways to deal with problems.

G

1. If somebody deliberately takes another person's life, they have no right to live.
2. Most killers act in the heat of the moment.
3. Violence and killing are ways to deal with problems.

H

1. Between murder rates in states that have the death penalty and those that don't.
3. By sentencing murderers and terrorists to death.
5. They sometimes have the right to take other human beings' lives.

Unit assessment

A

1. evidence   2. alibi   3. innocent
4. sentenced   5. violent   6. consideration
7. right   8. rate   9. arrested
10. serves

D

1. A witness identified her through a computer search.
2. He was branded as a criminal for a few years.
3. If somebody deliberately takes another person's life, they have no right to live.
4. The death penalty tells every member of society that it's OK to take another human being's life.
5. The two companies have agreed to settle out of court.

G

Word search
innocent, evidence, suspicion, convicted, criminal, motive, alibi, prosecuted, branded, murderer, deliberately, consequences, protect, sentenced, witness

H

Hidden message
Dear Nazim,
I was questioned by the police yesterday. They suspected I'd stolen a chicken from the supermarket and said they had evidence. They were just going to arrest me when I told them I own the supermarket. Manosh

UNIT 6

Listening/Reading Worksheet

B

1. set   2. spend   3. survive
4. that

Teacher's Book Answers

D

ozone, deforestation, ecosystem, exaggerating, survive

E

1. 8: dealing, deforestation, developed, don't, do, drastic, die, damaged
2. the near future
3. get together
4. permanently
5. It's not as bad as all that.

F

1. He thinks the United Nations should set up an organization to deal with environmental problems.
2. It may not survive much longer.
3. She is sure there will be progress on protecting the environment in the near future.

G

1. This organization would be responsible for dealing with problems.
2. The polar ice caps will melt.
3. More progress will be made in the near future.

H

1. The new organization would be responsible for dealing with problems like the thinning of the ozone layer and deforestation.
3. The world's ecosystem will be permanently damaged.
5. All countries need to get together.

Unit assessment

A

1. warming	2. side	3. forests
4. up	5. ozone	6. all
7. together	8. adapt	9. breathtaking
10. molehill		

D

1. Even if we cut down on carbon dioxide, it won't make much difference.
2. We may have permanently destroyed the Earth's ecosystem.

3. To stand any chance at all we have to radically change our way of life.
4. If we don't do something, many people will die of cancer caused by too much ultra-violet radiation.
5. This is just the tip of the iceberg – things are going to get worse.

G

Word search

warming, greenhouse, organic, breathtaking, ozone, ecosystem, emissions, permanently, drastic, exaggerating, habitat, iceberg, toxic, pesticide, consumerism

H

Hidden message
Dear Carlos,
The harvest was bad because of global warming. There's nuclear waste under one of our fields. And acid rain is destroying our crops. But it's wonderful on our farm! We have a breathtaking view of the polluted river. Abena

UNIT 7

Listening/Reading Worksheet

B

1. planet	2. years	3. sightings
4. evidence		

D

evidence, sightings, beings, insignificant, astronomers, advanced

E

1. 9: so, small, signs, some, should, sure, sightings, secret, society
2. UFOs
3. arrogant
4. keep, knowledge
5. life, beings

F

1. It's arrogant to assume we are the only intelligent beings.

2. They keep their evidence of UFOs secret.

3. Because her government is democratic.

G

1. The earth is just one small insignificant planet.
2. If there are intelligent aliens, some of them should have visited us by now.
3. There are so many reported sightings of UFOs.

H

1. They should have visited us by now.
3. There are many reported sightings of UFOs.
5. She thinks governments wouldn't keep their knowledge secret in a democratic society.

Unit assessment

A

1. light   2. support   3. enable
4. assume   5. astronomers 6. sightings
7. secret   8. solar   9. remain
10. guess

D

1. Astronomers will have to identify planets that can support human life.
2. It must sound like I read too many detective stories.
3. The government probably thinks we're not ready to know what's really going on.
4. I couldn't express myself very well, but that's what I was trying to say.
5. The exploration of space must continue whatever happens.

G

Word search
dimension, universe, sightings, astronomer, overcome, technology, assume, alien, solar, mystery, outer, saucer, reported, knowledge, exploration

H

Hidden message
Dear Chen
I've been in a flying saucer! Aliens abducted me

and took me at the speed of light into outer space. We even visited another dimension. They brought me back when they found I wasn't the American President. Annan

UNIT 8

Listening/Reading Worksheet

B

1. ordinary   2. place   3. more
4. me

D

tradition, humane, legal, suffering, senseless, sweeping

E

1. 6: legal, law, leader, like, leaders, live
2. just as
3. controlled
4. a sweeping statement
5. basis

F

1. He could remember the names of ordinary soldiers.
2. She is famous for starting a great nursing tradition.
3. Because they are leaders in a society created by men.

G

1. Napoleon could remember the names of ordinary soldiers.
2. Florence Nightingale started a great nursing tradition.
3. Female leaders have often been just as aggressive as male leaders.

H

1. She took care of the suffering caused by male generals and politicians.
3. If countries had been run by women like Florence Nightingale, there wouldn't have been any wars.
5. Having more of our society controlled by women.

Teacher's Book Answers

Unit assessment

A

1. feudal
2. aristocracy
3. industrial
4. colonies
5. legal
6. sweeping
7. course
8. difficult
9. break
10. matter

D

1. It would have been wonderful to see the feudal system being challenged.
2. Most aristocrats were constantly caught up in wars with other countries.
3. Generals and admirals are responsible for so much killing and suffering.
4. There wouldn't be any wars in the first place if countries were run by women.
5. It is often believed that the threat of war is an effective deterrent.

G

Word search

ancient, renaissance, feudal, revolution, medieval, period, innovation, colonies, tradition, sweeping, senseless, reformation, aristocracy, civilization, ordinary

H

Hidden message

Dear Christina,
If I was living in the medieval period I'd be a knight in shining armor. I'd be very brave and fight to reform the feudal system so all people could be equal. Everybody would say I was a good knight. Good night! Carlos

UNIT 9

Listening/Reading Worksheet

B

1. expect
2. pay
3. conditioned
4. better

D

discrimination, attention, positions, harassment, convenient, supposed

E

1. 6: hard, have, housework, having, happy, harassment
2. top
3. same, thinking
4. realized
5. pay attention to

F

1. They expect women to do the housework and take care of children even when they have full-time jobs.
2. They are happy to support their male bosses or pay more attention to their families.
3. She thinks it's hard for women to get to the top.

G

1. Women are supposed to be equal to men.
2. Many women are often happy to pay more attention to their families.
3. Women are conditioned to not want responsibility from the moment they are born.

H

1. They don't have the same opportunities as men.
3. Women without responsible jobs are happy to support their male bosses or pay more attention to their families.
5. Women trying to get to the top.

Unit Assessment

A

1. dominated
2. genetically
3. affirmative
4. most
5. support
6. convenient
7. conditioned
8. window
9. place
10. dogs

D

1. People talk about equal opportunity, but in fact men have all the power.
2. We need affirmative action to ensure there's a quota of female managers.
3. Many women who don't have responsible jobs pay more attention to their families.
4. There's a lot of sexual harassment and discrimination along the way.

5. If I play my cards right, I'll become my boss' right-hand woman.

G

Word search
supposed, harassment, conditioned, dominated, affirmative, quota, sexist, equally, support, innuendo, chauvinist, acceptable, appropriate, genetically, illusion

H

Hidden message
Dear Jin-Sook,
I was conditioned to accept a male-dominated working environment. My boss was a male chauvinist and there were no opportunities for female employees. To make things worse, my boss was my husband. Francesca

UNIT 10

Listening/Reading Worksheet

B
1. barriers   2. makes   3. benefits
4. harm

D
capital, protect, barriers, benefits, export, prevents, compete

E
1. 5: grow, globally, give, goods, good
2. prevents
3. aid, jobs
4. goods
5. import

F
1. It prevents developing countries from being able to compete globally.
2. It makes it easier for wealthier countries to provide aid to developing countries.
3. They move their factories to other countries.

G
1. Free trade prevents developing countries from being able to protect their industries.

2. A strong world economy benefits everybody.
3. As soon as local salaries increase too much, they move their factories to other countries.

H
1. She thinks free trade widens the gap between rich and poor.
3. He thinks investment in factories provides well-paid jobs.
5. She thinks countries giving aid do more harm than good.

Unit Assessment

A
1. forces   2. riddled   3. back
4. revitalizing 5. trade   6. benefits
7. harm   8. emergency   9. charity
10. nothing

D
1. The government does little to reduce poverty and hunger.
2. Developing countries should focus on reducing government corruption.
3. Free trade prevents countries from being able to protect their industries.
4. When local salaries increase too much, multinationals move their factories.
5. All the proceeds from their latest album will go to charity.

G
Word search
refugee, corruption, charity, hunger, administer, riddled, revitalizing, donate, ignore, appeal, poverty, bureaucracy, benefit, barrier, developing

H
Hidden message
Dear Manosh,
So many people are dying from hunger or are in need of aid. It sometimes seems that little of what we donate actually gets through to those who need it. But every little bit helps. We have to keep trying. Abena

Teacher's Book Answers

UNIT 11

Listening/Reading Worksheet

B
1. out   2. amount   3. crime
4. says

D
aggression, physical, prove, irresponsible, suicides, message, outlet, televised

E
1. 15: and, a, all, argument, are, also, accept, amount, an, act, as, aggression, after, about, any
2. sports, crime, movies
3. certain amount
4. send out
5. gives heavy publicity

F
1. They send out a message that it's all right to fight and hit people.
2. He thinks Tomoko would find it difficult to prove her argument.
3. He thinks the media is responsible for sensationalizing violence in physical sports.

G
1. Boxing and wrestling send out a message that it's all right to fight and hit people.
2. There's going to be a certain amount of violence in society whatever we do.
3. If the media didn't sensationalize violence, there wouldn't be any problem.

H
1. She thinks there'd be fewer wars.
3. He thinks sports provide an outlet for violence.
5. He thinks it should be blamed for the negative effects of violent sports.

Unit Assessment

A
1. society   2. blood   3. surrounded
4. models   5. vandalism 6. certain
7. sensationalize 8. resort   9. prepared
10. business

D
1. Every day we hear news of murders and hostages being taken.
2. We find it so violent because most of us live peaceful law-abiding lives.
3. Violent sports send out a message that it's all right to fight and hit people.
4. Sports can act as a substitute for aggression and war.
5. If our boss rejects our offer, we'll have a fight on our hands.

G
Word search
vandalism, revenge, serial, threaten, hostage, victim, commit, outwardly, banned, outlet, substitute, shocking, escalating, aggressive, televised

H
Hidden message
Dear Tomoko,
Violence and aggressive behavior are increasing all the time. Last night my boyfriend was threatened by a young girl! She said she would shoot him if he didn't date her! At least, that's what he told me.
Christina

UNIT 12

Listening/Reading Worksheet

B
1. every   2. change   3. freedom
4. sense

D
crisis, radical, complacent, elect, contentious, represented, anticipate

E
1. 11: country, change, comfortable, complacent, corrupt, communist, compromise, contentious, crisis, controlled, career
2. anticipate
3. radical

4. corrupt
5. contentious

F
1. Every four or five years.
2. There must be freedom of the press and freedom of speech.
3. A major world crisis.

G
1. Extremists keep moderates on their toes.
2. The system Annan's suggesting would lead to sensible compromises.
3. Everything would be controlled by career politicians and bureaucrats.

H
1. They often become complacent and corrupt.
3. They tend to be the most corrupt.
5. She feels Annan's idea is not inspiring enough.

Unit Assessment

A
1. represent   2. sake   3. sums
4. change   5. contentious   6. inspiring
7. entitled   8. policy   9. back
10. credit

D
1. Both left wing and right wing politicians seem so different from ordinary people.
2. When political parties are comfortable, they often become corrupt and complacent.
3. It would work as long as there was freedom of speech.
4. I doubt if the politicians would be able to deal with a major world crisis.
5. The recent election campaign was touch and go until the very end.

G
Word search
moderate, campaign, extremist, represent, consumed, dynamic, complacent, communist, compromise, contentious, alternative, anticipate, ideology, inspiring, ambition

H
Hidden message
Dear Annan,
I'd like to be President. I'm not left or right wing. I'm not an extremist or an idealist. I'm not even a moderate. In fact, I have no strong political opinions at all. So I think I'd represent a lot of people.
Tomoko

UNIT 13

Listening/Reading Worksheet

B
1. fall   2. put   3. effect
4. run

D
boost, reduced, progressive, demand, profitable, factors, slightly

E
1. 8: income, increase, increases, in, inflation, it, immediate, indirect
2. cause
3. fall
4. slightly
5. income tax

F
1. Because production will increase and unemployment will fall.
2. Because it leads to an increase in inflation.
3. Because poor people pay less progressive income tax than rich people.

G
1. Both these factors lead to an increase in inflation.
2. If GNP is higher, the government will get more income from indirect taxes.
3. Inflation hurts the poor more than the rich.

H
1. There is pressure to increase pay.
3. She thinks it would benefit the economy.
5. She thinks income taxes should be increased.

Teacher's Book Answers

Unit Assessment

A

1. growth   2. deficit   3. product
4. consumption 5. immediate   6. indirect
7. recession   8. pleasure   9. rebate
10. means

D

1. The government should boost productivity so as to stimulate economic growth.
2. The market research I've seen indicates there's little demand for our products.
3. The economy may improve but inflation will rise slightly in the long term.
4. Progressive income taxes affect the rich more than the poor.
5. The price of the tickets is high, but you'll definitely get your money's worth.

G

Word search

inflation, recession, indirect, market, productivity, consumption, deficit, trade, stimulate, unemployment, factors, progressive, profitable, rebate, export

H

Hidden message
Dear Jin-Sook
If consumption increases, it will boost economic growth and reduce the trade deficit. The government will then increase tax to prevent inflation, so consumption will decrease and we'll be back where we started. Nazim

UNIT 14

Listening/Reading Worksheet

B

1. better   2. last   3. find
4. world

D

wide, direction, surrounded, senses, whole, while, satisfied

E

1. 8: island, idea, improving, isn't, in, immediate, improve, it
2. raise
3. surrounded by
4. for a while
5. many, different, finding

F

1. Living on a romantic Pacific island isn't enough for Nazim.
2. We don't need to sit in an office to find a purpose in life.
3. He thinks they are not wide enough.

G

1. Tomoko wishes she could live forever on a romantic Pacific island.
2. Nazim feels he'd be wasting his life on a romantic island.
3. Tomoko thinks Nazim could raise a happy family on the island.

H

1. Living on a romantic Pacific island.
3. lying on a beach, eating exotic food, dancing all night, painting beautiful pictures, building a dream house, raising a happy family
5. He wants to improve society as a whole.

Unit Assessment

A

1. looking   2. satisfied   3. make
4. nothing   5. raise   6. whole
7. being   8. memory   9. generous
10. change

D

1. He doesn't feel deeply satisfied by anything he does.
2. I keep telling myself things can only get better.
3. My idea of happiness is to live on a romantic island.
4. Those ways of living are too concerned with the immediate world around us.
5. I have mixed feelings about moving away from New York.

G

Word search

inhibited, fulfilling, achievement, satisfied, complain, surrounded, direction, paradise, concerned, ending, mood, senses, situation, forever, immediate

H

Hidden message

Dear Abena,

My work is fulfilling, I think positively and make the most of every opportunity that comes my way, and I'm deeply satisfied by my personal life. But I'm very unhappy. I have no more goals in life. Chen

UNIT 15

Listening/Reading Worksheet

B

1. feet   2. ways   3. advantage
4. reach

D

advantage, nationalistic, questioning, straightforward, across, deeper

E

1. 13: stimulated, seeing, since, so, still, straightforward, seem, same, school, students, society, system, succeed
2. come across
3. fundamentals
4. in the first place
5. straightforward

F

1. They come across as uninternational.
2. Educating students about the world.
3. It dampens it down.

G

1. If he hadn't traveled, Chen would probably still have a nationalistic view of the world.
2. Some people who have traveled a lot come across as being very uninternational.
3. We are born with flexible and curious minds.

H

1. Seeing the world.
3. People who have never been abroad.
5. We have the potential to be full members of the international community.

Unit Assessment

A

1. outlook   2. ways   3. informed
4. feet   5. run   6. across
7. key   8. view   9. perfect
10. sorts

D

1. Some cultures are being suppressed by standardized global perspectives.
2. Even experts' opinions often seem to be based on prejudice and stereotypes.
3. I'm grateful to everybody who got me interested in traveling in the first place.
4. Some people who have never traveled come across as being very international.
5. We need to question fundamentals in order to reach our full potential.

G

Word search

stereotype, perspective, cosmopolitan, homogeneous, background, melting, ethnic, outlook, impression, itchy, flexible, community, advantage, dampens, potential

H

Hidden message

Dear Francesca,

I live in a multi-racial cosmopolitan city where ethnic minorities are tolerated and most people have an international outlook. But, personally I have many prejudices. I guess it takes all sorts to make a world. Carlos